TITANIA'S NUMBER

Titania Hardie

For Gavrik

A CONNECTIONS EDITION
This edition published in Great Britain in 2007 by
Connections Book Publishing Limited
St Chad's House, 148 King's Cross Road, London WC1X 9DH
www.connections-publishing.com

British Library Cataloguing-in-Publication data available on request.

ISBN 978-1-85906-228-9

1 3 5 7 9 10 8 6 4 2

Phototypeset in Bliss and Natural Script using QuarkXPress on Apple Macintosh
Printed in China

Contents

STARTING THE JOURNEY

This little book of numerology invites you to be amazed by what you will learn from numbers – about your character, your tastes, your instincts, your relationships, and even about your future. But to do this involves a willingness to believe – as Pythagoras, the 'Father of Numbers' did – that numbers can provide a clue, or formula, through which we can perceive some of the evolving patterns and cycles that affect our own individual existence. Let's find out more ...

Discovering numerology

Fans of Sudoku will understand how it entices us intellectually to see how strands of numbers – almost magically – slot together and interconnect with one another, revealing a rhythm of harmonious relationships between the lines. In one sense, numerology does this for us on a personal and spiritual level. The Science of Numbers, as it is called, suggests that there is an order and a rhythm in the universe of which we are a part, and although there is a certain mystery in the way numbers seem to function as symbols for our experiences, there is a long tradition across many cultures of their fascination for us.

Now, in an age of gigabytes, PINs and mathematic-based technology, how can we doubt the role that numbers play, or the way in which they have become part of our daily landscape? Numbers speak to us every day about our personal identity on this planet. Our birth date is absorbed by society as proof of our existence: you need it to be 'real' at the bank, in the office, when you travel, in an automated phone queue – in *all* official records. Indeed, many people consider the day-date of their birthday to be their lucky number. But can it really say anything about us?

Did you know, for instance, that:

- If you were a **5** or a **9**, you'd need to invest in good-quality luggage because you'd be bound to notch up a lot of air miles?
- Or that a **4** will painstakingly spend hours getting something just right, whereas a **1** will rush in and get several projects started, full of enthusiasm, only to leave someone else to carry them through to completion?
- And a **3** is a born entertainer, who enjoys spending time with others, whereas a **2** prefers to live quietly,

with just one or two partnerships, both socially and in business?

But you've picked *this* little volume because you're a **6**, which means that, being creative and kind to others, you probably feel compelled to generously host open-house for family and friends, whereas a **7** will be choosy about their company and guard their privacy more ... and an **8** would rather take everyone out to lunch on their bill!

About this book

Each individual title in this series investigates, in depth, the meaning of one of nine personal numbers. *This* volume is dedicated to the exploration of the number **6**.

We will be focusing principally on your **DAY** number – that is, the number relating to the day of the month on which you were born (in your case, the 6th, 15th or 24th of the month). Calculating your **DAY** number is easy: you simply add the digits of your day together (where applicable), and keep adding them until they reduce to a single number (*see calculation examples on page 270*). And that's it. It doesn't matter which month or year you were born in – you just need the day-date to discover your **DAY** number. And *you're* a **6.**

Your **DAY** number reveals all kinds of information, and, working from this number, we will be considering:

- The obvious attributes of your number as they impact on your personality
- How you are likely to dress, and what colours or styles appeal
- How you react to things psychologically, and what drives or motivates you
- In which fields you will have the most natural abilities and gifts

- What annoys you most
- What sort of lover you are, and how you relate to all other numbers
- What the future holds

... and much, much more.

And you have another significant number too: your **LIFE** number. This is derived from adding up the digits in the *whole* of your birth date – day, month and year (*see examples on page 270*). What does *this* number mean, and what do your **DAY** and **LIFE** numbers mean in tandem? And how does it affect you if you're also a 'master' number (**11** or **22**)? Read on and you'll see. But first, let's meet your **DAY** number ...

So, you're a 6

6

Considerate to your friends and at times too **kind-hearted**, you are an **artistic** soul with a wonderful eye for colour and harmony, and you love music and the visual arts in almost any expression. Though more of a **traditionalist** than a modernist, you nevertheless appreciate the avant-garde, and will always try to see what is special or aesthetically interesting about any piece of art, or space or building. You admire line and love to see an uplifting use of light, and you yourself are likely to have much talent as – at the very least – an amateur **musician** or singer, or **designer** of some sort. Mostly, too, **6**'s are **excellent cooks**, and play host to those they love on a frequent basis.

The number **6** often carries with it a great deal of

responsibility for others, especially family, and you may feel as though you can never be completely selfish with your time or your wants, always aware of the needs of those you care about. This can sometimes be a **burden**, but you have more **patience** than most numbers and often bear your duties with **grace**. You also have the kind of personality that is **naturally healing** – literally, the sound of your voice and the way that you speak may have a soothing effect on others. You are a good natural therapist and probably have a way with children, and you love to make your guests and friends feel welcome all the time, and will take trouble and care to offer them an ear when they need someone just to listen without judgement. That said, you do have excellent **analytical strengths** that enable you to see right to the heart of a problem.

The atmosphere of the family home is vitally important to a young **6**, and it may be that you have often cocooned yourself from harsh noise or argument, **retreating** into your own world. **6**s crave **peace**, and the kind of home they have is worth a huge investment of their time. You may well, therefore, be the one who always takes the trouble to see that there is plenty of everything – everyday **luxury** being something of a necessity to **6**. In our current cultural climate, a **6** will have paid attention to the scent, texture and comfort of their home space – and this is just as true of **6** men as **6** women. **6** men are more likely to settle and want children than almost any other number.

The most negative traits of this lovely, **gentle** number often arise because of **frustration**. That need for peace and calm sometimes prevents you from sallying forth into the world and demanding an outlet for your exceptional talents. You are able and widely gifted, but **not usually aggressive**. Then, too, if life seems to have asked you to become a **slave** to those who place demands on you, you may be more **obstinate** and inflexible than you might otherwise be. **6** does dig its heels in, but often more as a statement about security and the 'devil you know'. When you see the sense of gentle change, all is usually well.

One terrible tendency for an **over-burdened 6** is to lapse into martyrdom, or to allow yourself to **sacrifice** your entire life in some notion that it is for the good of someone else. This clips **6**'s naturally **creative** wings and prevents you from being the whole person you are. But it is more usual for a **6** to be **joyous** and loving, **sensitive** to others' feelings, good with people, and **a delight to visit**! You have the power to bring hope and pleasure, gentleness and joy, to anyone dear to you who has lost their way. Perhaps not as buoyant as **3**, you nevertheless gently **uplift** everyone around you. **Protective** and loyal, you have much kindness of spirit, which you put back into an often unkind world.

For the best chance of happiness and success, you should see to your education in artistic and aesthetic subjects. The more **effort** you put into your training and the more you broaden your knowledge about people and life, the greater the **reward** you will enjoy. You have a natural impulse to see a glass as **half-full** rather than half-empty, and making your own luck – with effort spent honing your talents and **pursuing your dreams** – should enable you to create a potentially **happy** world and lifestyle. Love – the affairs of your heart – will always be crucial to you, too.

Sound familiar? Getting a taste for what your number is about? And this is just the beginning. You'll soon find out how the number 6 expresses itself as your Day number in each and every day of your life. But before we go any further, let's take a look at where all this first came from . . .

What's in a number?

Numbers have always had a sacred meaning. The Egyptians used an alphabet that conflated letters and numbers, and, as such, each number exuded an idea that was more than the sum it stood for. There is a whole book of the Old Testament devoted to the subject; and the Hebrew language – exactly like the Egyptian – has a magical subtext of meaning where letters and numbers can be doubled to reveal an extra layer of secret, so-called 'occult' information. It is called the *gematria*, and forms a crucial part of the sacred occult wisdom called Kabbalah. There were twenty-two letters – a master number – in both the Greek (Phoenician) and Hebrew alphabets, and repetitions of the spiritual properties of the numbers **3** and, especially, **7** recur throughout the Bible.

The Father of Numbers

But modern numerology derives more formally from Pythagoras, the Father of Numbers, who was a serious and spiritual philosopher, as well as the man who explained some of the secrets of geometry. Born on the island of Samos, although he ultimately settled in Cretona, a Greek colony in southern Italy, he is understood to have travelled widely to both Egypt and Judea. Some accounts of his life also suggest he may have studied under the Persian sages of Zoroaster, but an analysis of his teachings certainly reveals the strong influence of Kabbalistic thought in his philosophy.

Pythagoras understood numbers as a *quality* of being, as well as a *quantity* of material value. In one sense, the numbers as figures were connected with the measuring of things, but 'number' itself was significantly different to this, and encompassed a spiritual value. The numbers from one through to nine represented universal principles through which everything evolves, symbolizing even the stages an idea passes through before it becomes a reality. Mathematics was the tool through which we could apprehend the Creation, the universe, and ourselves. Musical harmony was a sacred part of this knowledge, as was geometry, which revealed divine proportion.

Most importantly, Pythagoras believed that numbers were expressive of the principles of all real existence – that numbers themselves embodied the principles of our dawning awareness, our conjecture and growth. Through mathematics and number we could approach divine wisdom and the workings of the universe as a macrocosm. Thus, in microcosm, our personal 'mathematics' would unlock the workings of our own being, and help us to see a divine wisdom concerning ourselves. **1** was not just the first digit, but also had a character of beginning, of independence, of leadership, just as the number **2** was more than merely the second number quantifying two objects, but also implied the philosophical concept of a pair, of co-operation, of a relationship beyond the individual.

Pythagoras also believed that we could understand our direction and fate through an awareness of repeating cycles of number, making numerology a key to revealing our opportunities and our destiny.

By tradition, the doctrine Pythagoras taught to his students in the sixth century BCE was secret, and no one wrote down his ideas until his death. But Plato was a follower of Pythagoras and, along with the rebirth of Platonism, the ideas of the Father of Mathematics were revealed afresh during the revival of Greek learning in the Renaissance. The great magi of the fifteenth and sixteenth centuries explored anew the significance of number and the gematria, to understand the hidden messages of the ancients and of the divine mind. Mathematics as a philosophy was the bridge to higher realms of spirituality.

Essence of the numbers

one is the spark, the beginning, Alpha, the Ego of consciousness. It is male.

two is consort. Adding partnership, receptivity, it is female, bringing tact.

three is a synthesizing of both of these qualities and brings expansion and joy.

four is the number of the Earth, of the garden, and of stability. It brings order.

five is curiosity and experiment, freedom, changes. It brings sensuality.

six nurtures and cares for others. It will love and beautify, and brings counsel.

seven perfects and contemplates the Creation. It is intellect, stillness, spirit.

eight is the number of power, the octave, a higher incarnation. It brings judgement.

nine is humanity, selflessness, often impersonal and all-knowing. It brings compassion.

Applying the knowledge

A deeper understanding of the self can be achieved through an awareness of the mysticism of number within us; and both the birth date and, to some degree, our given name are the keys to unlocking our mystical, spiritual core of being. Exploring the affinity between letter and number can also reveal insights about the lessons we need to learn throughout our lives to improve and develop as individuals (*see page 25*).

This book looks at the significance of numbers as they affect us every day, focusing largely, as introduced earlier, on our **DAY** number. It is this number that reveals to us our instincts, our impulses, our natural tastes and undiluted responses, our talents and immediate inclinations. This is how people see us in daily situations, and how we behave by essence.

We will be exploring how our **DAY** number influences

our love relationships and friendships; at what it says about our career strengths and our childhood; at the way our number manifests in our leisure time; and at how it might give us a better understanding of what to expect in our future cycles, as we pass through any given year under the sway of a particular number. Each birthday initiates a new cycle, and each cycle seems uncannily connected with the philosophical concerns of the number which governs that year. Look both to the past and present to see how strongly the number-cycle can illuminate our experiences ... and then count ahead to ponder what may be in store over the next year or two.

And numbers also say something about where we live or work, about our car, and even about our pets. Understanding these secret qualities can add a new dimension of pleasure – not to mention surprise – to our journey through life.

A NUMBER TO GROW INTO

The presence of our **LIFE** number, however, takes longer for us to appreciate in ourselves – longer for us to grow into – and it often takes time to reveal itself. This number comes to the fore as your life progresses, and on pages 214–247 we will be looking at the meaning of your **DAY** number together with your individual **LIFE** number, to see what this reveals about your character and potentiality.

The **LIFE** number may intensify the experience of the **DAY** number – if it is closely related to it, or shares similar patterns. But more frequently our two different numbers clash a little, and this often allows insight into the aspects of our being where instinct pulls us in one direction but higher wisdom or experience mediates and pulls us in a second direction.

Who would have thought you could learn so much from a number? Pythagoras certainly did, over 2,500 years ago ... and now you will discover it too.

What's in a name?

Your name also has a story to tell, and it is a story revealed through number. Every letter corresponds to a number: in the Western alphabet we use twenty-six letters, which are at variance with the twenty-two formerly enshrined in the Hebrew and Greek alphabets. Some numerologists believe that this is in keeping with the more material world we now live in, as the number '26' reduces to '8' (when you add the digits), which is the number of power and money.

The correspondences between the numbers and the letters of the alphabet are as follows:

1	2	3	4	5	6	7	8	9
A	B	C	D	E	F	G	H	I
J	K	L	M	N	O	P	Q	R
S	T	U	V	W	X	Y	Z	

As you are a **6**, it is most revealing to look at the letters F, O and X as they occur (or not!) in your name. This is because they intensify the experience and impression of your main number.

To make the most of the qualities inherent in your number, you should be using a name which is in poetic harmony with your **DAY** number. As a **6**, you will be at your most artistic and serene every day, and will also satisfy your need to be loved, if you have a name which underlines these lovely **6** qualities. Using a name which includes an F, O or X bolsters your powers. If this sounds strange, consider that many of us have our names shortened or played upon by friends, family and lovers, so it is important to feel that our chosen name – the one that we use as we go about in the world – is making the best of our abilities and energies.

Among the letters that are equivalent to the number **6**, O is a common vowel – so the chances are that you have this letter in your name. It is especially significant if your name starts with an O, or if it's the first vowel in your name, because this strengthens the beauty of your **6** at the beginning of your name. Create a nickname with it in, if necessary, just to back up the outstanding properties of artistic ability that come with your number.

The letter-numbers help us to act out our sense of purpose, and if these work in correspondence with the **DAY** number we are more likely to find our sense of will and achieve our goals more rapidly. But if we have few, or none, of the letters of our **DAY** number, we often feel it is much harder to shine in our field of opportunity.

Missing a '6' letter?

As a **6**, you rely on demonstrating your feelings to others, but if you have no '**6**' letters in your name you may be finding it harder to ask for what you want in relationships, or you might be unable to settle comfortably into any kind of domesticity.

6 rules heart and home so completely that a lack of this letter/number in your name (or nickname) often makes you feel undeserving of love – or even doubt that you will truly be loved. It's vital that you find a way to work a '**6**' letter into your life – as a company name or pet name, for instance, or by playing with the spelling of your name. Then you will gain confidence about the way the world sees and responds to you.

Too many '7's or 'O's?

It can be just as much of a problem if your name carries a flood of letters which correspond to your number. While a lack of 'O's could make you something of a sinner, a surfeit could make you too much of a saint! More than three will add an extra degree of obstinacy, while a large number of 'F's might make you sad through too much compassion for others. Watch your nerves and attend to your health if you have several of either of these letters.

6 indulges in luxury foods and company, and too many '**6**' letters can lead to overeating, or to you failing to pay adequate attention to your fitness. You may also worry about love matters too much – and to the exclusion of any balance! Try to choose a name for everyday use that minimizes the number of '**6**' letters.

YOUR DAY NUMBER

It's a new day ...

You will learn a lot about the numbers of your birthday and your name as this book unfolds, but the DAY number is, to my mind, the most important – and sometimes least well-recognized – number of all ... the number which exerts a magnetic hold on us each and every day of our lives. Every time we react to a situation, an emotion, a provocation of any kind, we are shooting straight from the hip, as it were, and this reaction is coloured by our DAY number.

As we know, your 'Day Force', or **DAY**, number is **6** if you were born on the 6th, 15th or 24th of any month. Each of these different dates also affects us – the characteristics of the number derived from a birthday on the 15th vary intriguingly from one on the 24th, for instance – and we will look at these differences in the pages ahead.

All three dates, however, still reconcile to an overall **6**. This number determines your gut reactions and the way you express yourself when you are being most true to yourself. Your parents, lovers, friends and co-workers all know you best through this number.

So what is the theme of being a 6? What are you like when you're at work, rest and play? And how compatible are you with the other numbers? Let's find out ...

6'S CHARACTER

Charms, graces, warts and all ...

Surrounded by an air of calm authority and serenity, and giving the impression that your feet only just touch the ground, you are one of the most giving and delightful numbers in the pantheon. 6s have a gentle and unforced style, respond well to objects that are beautiful and people who are cultured, and like to create a sympathetic environment around them that is partly orchestrated for the pleasure of others too.

Inclined to symmetry and balance of line and colour, your number bathes you in a feeling for what is lovely in the world. Your chosen field really ought to be in the creative arts for you to express yourself fully and happily, and also because it is likely to bring you success and esteem.

Truly blessed

This is a **DAY** number which blesses you with concern for other people in the kindest way. Unless you exhibit every negative trait of the number and lack any positive connection, you are happy for others' joy and success, and regard good news for them as equally joyous for you – and this sincerity and goodness is felt by everyone who knows you. In fact, you don't like any show of jealousy in others, and can't understand why it should be so – but this level of idealism sometimes means you are let down by less generous souls!

Guided by your heart almost more than your head (although you are innately wise, too), you have strong principles and a good work ethic. This in itself makes you both useful to the community around you and lucky in the way the world treats you – for the most part. Even as a child you may have felt keenly what was right and what was wrong, and your natural grace and manners make others comfortable around you. Therefore, though you never give the impression of being forceful or ambitious, you find others willing to do your bidding, and you succeed without too much apparent push. Really, you make your own luck.

The sixth sense

You do love to earn well, because beautiful luxuries are a requisite part of your life – nor are you the person to give a cheap gift or forget someone's birthday, so money must be there for you to express your true nature. You are certainly intelligent, but your real knack is with *people*, at a gentle and reassuring level. This makes you the perfect teacher or healer, a good doctor, a kind counsellor, a warm social worker. Yet somehow, even if a **6** works in a scientific quarter, art will be close by: for instance, you may be a botanist who draws wonderful plants, or an archaeologist

Keynotes of the 6 personality

Positive associations: idealistic, hopeful about others, unselfish, extremely artistic, appreciative of aesthetics, lucky with money, wonderful home-maker, kind to all, creatively talented, peacemaker, loving

Negative associations: can be overly methodical, slow to react, one-track-minded, reclusive rather than hospitable, too caught up in other people's woes, prone to flattery, bogged down by family

who loves to record finds and draw ruins. There is certainly a romantic edge to your personality – even when you are being very practical!

Partly because of your affectionate nature and your gentleness, you are able to elicit the best behaviour from others all around you. You teach those you love, and whom you share a world with, to be harmonious with one another, and you carry an aura of your own world with you wherever you go. Your office is likely to reflect your taste (and even your love of scent!), and, when you travel, a part of your home and personal lifestyle is packed too. Luxury travel goods, grooming kits and bathrobe or stylish slip-ons are sure to be a priority in your overnight bag.

A taste for beauty

Your personal style is effortlessly graceful, if you are truly living out your number to its highest capacity. Harmonizing colours and style, yet not necessarily tied to an outfit designed to be teamed by its manufacturers, you blend items with classic flair, and make everything look good on you. **6**s are usually beautiful – even if they may sometimes carry just a little too much weight – and you probably have the skill to carry off some superb and artistically inspired combinations. Even male **6**s have a gentle 'peacockry' about them (though they are not desperately narcissistic), but all **6**s love to add beauty to the space they are occupying, and this includes their personal style.

Your home is probably very important to you, and many **6**s work from home, in one sense or another. Even if you have an office elsewhere, your **6** influence extends into the home environment and creates a chameleon space within a living area that is beautifully decorated and unobtrusive. You work hard – and you work hard at all things in order that others don't have to work so hard! But, on a cautionary note, **6**s can have a tendency to stifle others with too much help or too much love, or even too much expectation. You take such care of what you do for everyone, and are offended if this isn't appreciated at least a little bit.

The path to success

Even though your number gives an impression of lacking a killer instinct – which indeed it does – you do have a very acute business ability, and usually succeed in whichever career field you select. You are not the kind of person to pick a vocation based on its earning potential, but you need to feel 'at home' in everything you do, and this means you work to get things just so in your business life. Such attention brings dividends, and with so many talents at your fingertips you will soon be seen as someone who can turn their hand to nearly anything in their work life. Your reputation grows, and your opportunities with it.

And, quite apart from this, you have a knack with money, which usually manages to find you. This may come through a partner or through love relationships, or even because you adopt family so much – and so extensively – that you gain extra family members along the way in life. In any case, from the combination of work talent and opportunity, money is mostly fairly secure in your life path, and, if you have a bad patch, things generally come out well again before too long.

At your service

Responsibility is one of the things that is thrown at you often in your life – sometimes, when you least expect it. A **6** mum, for instance, whose children grow and flee from the home, may imagine herself ready at last to have time again to herself; yet this so often eludes her. Relatives, in-laws, other business necessities, older people – all arrive in different measure. At times, this can be a load to carry, but the truth is that **6**s usually carry it without feeling too much pain as a result. In fact, responsibility is more often a pleasure or a dignified task for you, because your number sees all forms of service to others as extended hospitality. There is beauty in such service and, if anyone can see that, it is you.

This can make you wise and patient, and it is this ability to conceptualize duty in such a way that makes **6**s the nurses, doctors, hospital and education workers, philosophers and instructors of our world. You may never learn the trick of separating your emotions from the job – but then you probably don't want to. And, where **9**s are a big brother to everyone, and become involved with large numbers of people at once, **6**s get involved at a personal level, one on one.

Dinner is served!

Have I ever met a **6** who doesn't like good food – or, indeed, know how to cook well? Not really! Even as children, **6**s will bake a little, or have a palate for food that is properly cooked and nicely presented.

A **6** who hasn't been exposed to culinary delights is a sad thing to imagine, because **6**s love to open their home and their pantry as soon as someone calls in unannounced. Casual and unexpected visitors never faze a **6**, who always has well-stocked cupboards, or a cake ready to pull from the freezer on the off-chance. And a **6** will have learned how to cook so well because they simply refuse point blank to eat badly. Many **6**s are restaurant owners (or have a share in a restaurant), or have jobs in chic catering outfits. Rule of thumb for others who eat with you is that you never eat badly chez **6**!

We looked earlier at the importance of having '**6**'

letters in your name: using a name containing the letters F, O or X will help you to develop and exude the most creative and loving aspects of your personality. Without any letter in your name to the value of **6**, your confidence may be lacking regarding your talents and self-worth. You may wish to be more beautiful or happier in love, always feeling you are failing to live up to the standard you expect from yourself.

If this is so, give yourself a new name, or a new way of spelling your old one, and start to enjoy your exceptional gifts. You have work to do, beautifying and healing the world – and those of us who live in it. But remember the caution: too many '**6**' letters – especially too many 'O's and 'F's combined – and you may find you are drawn to so many varying interests in the arts, or in music, that you become more of a dilettante than a specialist at any of them. Try to find one strong expression of your gifts and perfect it.

All you need is love

Your number is known as the number of love – and I have not yet said enough about this connection, and what it means for you. Like the planet Venus – which signifies our response to the arts and matters of beauty, and our relationships with the opposite sex in love – **6** as a number is connected with the dominion of this same goddess, and love and gentle sensuality are part of your deeper self.

A **6** child needs to be loved openly, and to have expressions of affection from the family in order to grow and thrive. And, in matters of the heart, **6** may be too trusting and give everything to an important early love, without reservation. If this is in any way not respected, accepted or reciprocated, a **6**'s memory is long and tender, and it will influence the way you think or act with others for years. And nothing is sadder than a loving **6** becoming too cautious to forge relationships.

It is important to select the 'true' from the 'false' in love affairs, and not to smother a loved one with your exceptionally deep well of affection. This may take some time to understand and practise – but never walk away from the gentle act of loving, otherwise you lose some of the very best of yourself.

Hope springs eternal

You are very protective of those around you – especially children – and you have a strong compulsion to do good things socially. Perhaps it is your appreciation for symmetry and balance which fires your social conscience and drives you to find some use for your time that benefits other people. If other members of the family, or friends, are living far away, it is *you* who remembers them and cheers them with regular contact. And so it is in the social world around you: the child who needs a little extra teaching support, or the young musician or artist who has talent, but lacks resources or confidence, is likely to become your protégé. Anywhere a **6** can add hope, that is where we will find you!

And daily, in your heart, you need to surround yourself with the people and the things that inspire your considerable gifts and gentleness. You respond to beauty, to peace, to kindness in others, and you need to keep this in the forefront of your mind, striving to create and maintain business and personal relationships that respect this need. Then you will soar and fulfil your best character traits, bringing sympathy and loyalty everywhere you go. Your presence can be a lift for everyone else around you: **6** is like a rainbow somehow breaking through the clouds on a grey day – a bridge of peace and a sign of better things to come!

Honest and frank with others, you are capable of saying what you mean to anyone, at the risk of being blunt and uncompromising if you think that something you see or feel is unjust. **6**s really are the loveliest people – and, as long as you don't become too single-minded in your outlook or belief system, you are a true helper and comforter to the world. **6** can be shy, but is really a gentle extrovert, and you may be happiest when you can find a niche that allows you at least a little public display and outward show of your talents.

That said – and as a final word here – **6** is never vulgar or brash. Yours is the number of proportion and good taste, and lucky people hold it.

6 in a nutshell

Personality watchwords: idealistic, unselfish, kind
Lucky colours: scarlet, mustard, heliotrope
Lucky herbs/flowers: red rose, sweet pea, iris, myrtle, lady's mantle
Scents: rose, galbanum, geranium
Fashion style: subtle colour, balanced line, classic cut and fabric
Decorative style: harmonious, preference for tradition, attention to detail
Letters: F, O or X (needed in the name you use)
Car style: quietly expensive rather than flashy, tactile upholstery, comfortable
Holiday destination: an island, or old-fashioned towns, from New England to Tuscany

Which 6 are you?

2 3 4 5 **6** 7 8 9 1

Everyone with a **DAY** number of **6** will exhibit many of the characteristics just discussed. It is interesting to see, though, how the number **6** varies across all of its incarnations. There is a subtle but definite difference between the way the number operates for someone born on the 6th of the month – which makes for a pure **6** effect – and someone born, say, on the 24th.

As a rule, anyone born on the single-digit date has the truest and most undiluted effect from the number, whereas someone born as a product of two digits borrows some qualities from the pairing of the numbers. Twenty-anything puts the softening digit '2' before the second number, and this usually means that, whatever number you are, you are more aware of the needs of others. Similarly, if '1' is the first digit (15th) you are more independent, and perhaps more assured of your self-worth, than other **6** people.

Let's look at the variations across all the birthdays ...

Born on the 6th?

With the pure form of this DAY number as your birthday, you are an especially artistic individual with a true need to surround yourself with beautiful things, and beautiful people, in your daily life. Music is a vital part of your relaxation, and your career should definitely be chosen from a creative field.

All people who are born on the 6th of any month have a deep love of nature, home, family and friends. In fact, with this birthday you have a strong concern for humanitarian issues. You want – and need – to love and be loved, and will seek approval from family, loved ones and co-workers. You'll be miserable if you feel neglected or unappreciated. You also gain a reputation for being the right person to settle differences between members of your family and your work peers.

This pure **6** birthday usually implies that its holder – male or female – will be an especially good cook, and you will probably never need to follow a recipe very closely, having a natural culinary instinct. You are imaginative, intuitive and creative, and you love to beautify all you touch. You will get on wonderfully with children of all ages, becoming one of them when you need to, thinking and feeling personally for the young and the old alike. You can create a magical environment, easily blending visual harmony with comfort. Just add a **3**, and you would be the perfect event organizer for children's parties or festivals!

You generously offer help wherever it is needed, but with this birthday it can mean that you're stubborn and argumentative at times, too. You have a powerful desire for a peaceful lifestyle, but this makes you fight for your beliefs against all-comers. Usually you will restore your own sweet-temperedness after a moment's reflection. Pure **6**s are especially gifted musically – though sometimes untrained – and often have a beautiful singing or speaking voice. You instinctively keep music playing constantly around you, and sing sweet songs while you work, and you also see things in visual terms in your daily life, whether at home or at the office. **6**s will decorate and embellish with very good taste.

Pure **6**s generally have a broad interest in group affairs, helping colleagues, neighbours and friends through difficult patches. You are a very good listener. Career-wise you would succeed in any field which engages your artistic eye or your sense of fashion and beauty, or which utilizes your ability to make people feel nurtured and cared about. You may have an interest in health and diet, and could work happily in this area. The music industry, interior design, graphics, the fashion industry (especially concerning accessories), fine art, restaurants and food, or any business working closely with and for women (remember Venus is your patron!), will be your forte. (We will be looking at career prospects in more detail shortly; *see page 62.*)

You have a very strong sense of smell, and respond powerfully to the scent of those you come into contact with. It is like an extra sense with you – one that tells you deep within whether things are 'right'. Born on the 6th, you may also be quite lucky with money.

Born on the 15th?

The 15th is a birthday for warm and loving people, and those born on this day have a quality of intense personal magnetism. With this particular 'Day Force' you will be a good friend and helpful associate to those close to you, and you have a talent for gentle persuasion and for being seen by everyone in your best light. A comfortable home – well accoutred with luxuries – is important to you, and to meet the need to earn such a home you are highly capable and independent. Yet, you always take the time required of you to help other people.

You gain a sense of genuine accomplishment from sorting out others' dilemmas. Conscious, as you are, of people's weaknesses and foibles, you are very forgiving of others' mistakes, and are understanding when things sometimes don't work out quite the way you would wish.

Nevertheless, you're not above taking advantage of people who act truly foolishly, and, more than other **6**, you step on the occasional toe when you are in pursuit of your own goals. Mostly, your charm sees to it that you are forgiven.

Similarly to those born on the 6th, if you have this birthday you will probably be an inspired and inventive cook, and a wonderful host to your guests. But, as much as owning or having a share in a restaurant may suit your bonhomie and skill, this may not be your ambition. You have other artistic arrows in flight, and you need to express several of your gifts at one time. You will certainly be happiest and most confident if you come from a happy home background, as this helps you to give full force to your loving, creative, romantic nature. You would make a superb teacher or parent – even, perhaps, to your own parents – and will be lucky enough to attract sincere friends, unexpected gifts, kind admiration and sudden opportunities. Yours is a number of good fortune.

An excellent student, and someone who misses little subtlety, you are a keen observer of human nature. Through this faculty you will absorb facts, gather knowledge and gain personal wisdom. Your understanding of life seems to come more from perception than from study and research, and people will rightly see you as empathetic and feeling. You exude an inexhaustible youth and vitality, and you are a buoyant companion.

It is very important for you to develop this sense of personal wisdom, for life occasionally throws tests at you – particularly concerning the material world. This may come in the form of relationships, where the lesson will be about the possible hollowness of material possessions. You will come to see luxury rewards and objects as transient pleasures which can just as easily make you a slave to obtain them. You may spend considerable time pondering the way in which human beings make unnecessary bonds for themselves over items not worth the human price. You have little time for those who only pursue the soft option but who cannot live with hard truths and stark realizations. Your own best outlet for the disappointment of human failing is through laughter and kindness to others, and – mostly – you manage this!

Perhaps you love to paint and make hand-crafted objects for your own enjoyment, as you are undoubtedly artistic and creative in so many spheres. You have an ear for music and a good singing and speaking voice, and you may have a taste for the opera even if it is not fashionable among your circle of friends. You are not afraid to go against accepted common taste, and you will say what you truly feel if you enjoy something. In business, any intellectual or artistic outlet will suit you very well and bring you fulfilment, particularly if you work in fashion, publishing, medicine, food, or with musical people, costume designers, interior stylists or in the beauty business. You may even teach at the highest level.

Born on the 24th?

This birthday is concerned with responsibility to others and a life where there is service and duty to loved ones, but it is usually also connected with personal longevity – so a time for you yourself should eventually come! You attract money in so many ways, and have an excellent chance of making a financial success of your life, provided you actualize your ideas and don't just dream about what you *could* do. You are also sure to receive money from others.

Your family is very important to you, right from childhood, and you will be a caring and inventive parent yourself. One of the warmest and most earnest companions a person could wish for, you enjoy your home and want to make it look and feel inviting and welcoming, to share with others. People with authority and influence come to you. You offer them wonderful hospitality, as you are an excellent cook, preferring not to rely on recipe books but picking up the odd tip as you go from place to place in your life.

You are good at communicating with very old or very young people. Sometimes this infers that you will have too much responsibility in caring for elderly members of your family, and long being affected by their needs and wishes, but you are usually generous and patient with anyone who needs your time. You may almost have a feeling of religious duty about the way you see your life, and you bear much because of this spiritual outlook.

Although you are elegant and rather regal in your bearing, you do have some surprisingly negative tendencies of jealousy and worry in relation to others, when you really have little need for it. Also, you can hardly help yourself from finding fault with people, partly because your critical facet is, in fact, almost as acute as that of a number **7**. You can be manipulative and terribly stubborn, which will surprise anyone who thinks you only have a gentle and benign face. This is partly because you can be very proud and quietly ambitious, and you don't like to be thwarted at all!

If, however, you make use of your positive talents, charms and considerable energies by remaining active, there is no limit to what you might accomplish. You are very talented in almost all of the creative departments of life, particularly with visual arts. You may speak or sing well, and it is important to consider that this vocal sweetness may mean you would be at an advantage if you pursue your goals in person or by telephone, rather than by e-mail or letter. You can usually talk someone around to what you want or need, with genuine charm and grace.

Your career gifts may reside in fashion, all areas of design, music, art and writing. You might choose to act, or simply to be in a position where you can do a lot of talking to others. This birthday brings the ability to make speeches and give addresses at gatherings, which you do without pretension. Others look to you time and again for a few well-chosen words.

Like all **6**s, you need and want to be loved - perhaps even a little too longingly. You may, however, fight your impulse to love, or doubt that anyone can meet the standard of emotion you feel you need to be happy. Try not to intellectualize this, and to go with your feelings more; but at the same time remember not to place too much onus on someone else's perfection. Love a *real* person, not an idealized one!

This birthday enjoys the vocational fields of creativity cited above and, in addition, banking, university or college teaching, the catering trade, sciences, and healing or therapy (more about careers follows shortly; *see page 62*). Money will come to you easily if you focus yourself.

6 AT WORK

So, what kind of employee does your number make you? We've already seen that your birthday suggests you are much more comfortable working in a close partnership, but when you are in a large group, how do you fit in? If you're the boss, are you a good one? Which fields are likely to be the best for your talents? And which the worst? And what about the male/female divide? Is a 6 female boss more desirable than a 6 male colleague?

Here, we get to grips with your career potential, your needs and 'must-have's for job satisfaction, and your loves and loathes work-wise, hopefully highlighting some areas where there is room for you to adjust your manner around others, to help you achieve what it is you're aiming for.

In the marketplace

Your number might be deemed the 'I balance' of numerology, rather like the astrological Air sign Libra, which is ruled by Venus. This means that, whether you are just starting out at work or are a seasoned professional, your mind is sensitive to how others are feeling and contributing, and that you are both wise and conscientious where your peers are concerned.

You have strongly ingrained principles about business ethics and conduct at the office, and if you say you can do something, you like to be reliable to all. Although **6** is rather a conservative number in many respects, your sense of justice means you are a gentle advocate of equal pay for men and women, and that you don't like exploitation of others. Everyone should be valued for whatever contribution they can make.

HARMONY RULES

Upholding conventions regarding manners and social politeness at work, you will always look for a harmonious way to achieve good career relationships, and will avoid discord with others at all costs. **6**s sometimes fail to be blunt with their workforce or co-workers simply because they don't want any bad feeling, and this means that unpleasant discussions may be put off entirely, or handed over to others. Curiously, this is in direct opposition to **6**'s love of honesty, but if an adjustment has to be made with others, **6** may take the easy path and inveigle others to do the dirty work – resulting in a hegemony if **6** is in control! And you take advantage of the fact that no one wants to upset or say 'no' to you: **6** is charming and kind, but not above being manipulative!

You love to work, and to be well-recognized and well-paid for what you do. You may also occasionally have a false sense of how much you bring to what you do, ignoring the input of fellow workers. This is not megalomania on your part so much as a wish to be involved at all levels of a project, and sometimes this brings with it an oversight about where an idea started, or how much leg work others have put in before it reached you! This notwithstanding, when you are driven by communal need you can be very selfless, and work longest and hardest to a common cause.

Your natural charm and ability with others, married to your intelligence and talent, usually means you are in a top job, or that you have a great deal of authority; but if your work is always of the hard and demanding physical variety, without proper remuneration, you may not have tapped into your true talents, or have trained to make full use of them.

WHERE DOES YOUR LIGHT REALLY SHINE?

Here are some of the qualities that **6**s bring to any job:

- A love of creating ease and making a difference would

place you at the top in any form of social work. Excellent people skills ensure you are the best person to liaise with in a client-based business, and if a go-between is needed between work and management or private business and public good, that person is highly likely to be a **6**.

- Reader, theatre-goer and lover of the arts, you adore days spent absorbed in your own thoughts exploring a gallery or museum, so if your work were connected with such interests it could become a source of happiness for you. This interest often fuels **6**s to work in media or publishing connected with the arts, allowing you to make the finest work appeal beyond a purely elite audience. Rather like **2**, **6** is a mitigator.
- No one will give more to a job than a **6**. Patient and feeling for others' woes, yours is the number best suited to healing professions, but even if you are working in an entirely different field, somehow the office first aid

or the school infirmary may also come under your care. Your ability to soothe everyone from a sick child to a grumpy boss is in your favour, and will see to your advancement.

- A wish to make luxury treats more of an everyday thing could be a goal that entices you to work in the high end of the food, hotel or catering markets. You would be perfectly content in an old-fashioned, smartly polished tea room, offering scrumptious cakes and rounds of sympathy, not to mention beautiful décor, to its customers. **6**s are wonderful proprietors in any businesses, ever attentive to their customers' needs and comfort, and food is a special area of expertise for a **6**.
- **6** does the humanitarian work on the planet – along with number **9** – and you will feel vindicated if you can contribute to anything which improves the lot of your fellow beings, or brings greater awareness of social or cultural ills to those around you. Even if your work is not

exactly in the humanitarian field, you will find yourself carrying out small, generous acts for those who work near to you or who are dependent on you in business.

Contriving aesthetic pleasures for those you have contact with, and finding a way of improving what is fair or just around you, are necessary elements in your work life. A **6**'s career can flourish in many and varied spheres, but these are the aspects requisite for happiness. You are sure to find a way to turn a taste for comfort, beauty and human ease into a work opportunity that could do extremely well for everyone. **6** has a nose for business, and these are some of the areas that could be of interest ...

The arts This is the most obvious starting point for someone with your taste and skills. Art forms a backdrop to your world, from the colour of your sheets to the blended tones on your desk and in your bathroom. A **6** can never be unaware of colour and line. You may be a born artist or promoter of the arts. All aspects of the arts culture are part of your instinctive make-up. Whether you want to choreograph a ballet or paint the scenes at the opera, **6** has talent in the visual arena, and is not a complete person until this has been unlocked.

Welfare work A drive toward idealism coupled with good application makes you feel the urge to work in a job that betters the community. Welfare work truly comes under the domain of **6**. Whether as a physician, a biochemist searching for improvements in the tools of medicine, or a psychologist concerned with smoothing out the anxieties of the mind, your number has a sense of mission about making the world an easier and more successful place for the human race to live.

And this extends to all god's creatures: **6**s love pets and make wonderful vets or workers with large animals.

Long hours simply aren't a problem for you, provided the work is uplifting.

Beauty/luxury industries Luxuries and assets that make life a little more comfortable are the things you love and the items you would like to provide for others. Businesses built around such things – the luxury goods trade, or high-quality designer items – are a perfect outlet for your talents. You have a head for business and the character for creating client goodwill as well. This often sees a **6** in control of their own company in a field which comes under the luxury/beauty banner.

Interior design/home improvement Because your vocational strengths come in any area where you enhance the human world and make people's lives more comfortable, work in (or concerning) the home is perfection for a **6**. Decorating or designing, styling or improving the home space is instinctive for you – and all the better if you can turn this to a business. The garden may also attract you – especially if you have the number **4** elsewhere in your numbers (such as your LIFE number; *see page 214*) – and, as a **6**, water features, or the sound of a nearby river, will be important. **6**s often work from home, too, and will beautify their workspace.

Pottery/commercial art These form the heart of a **6**'s industry. Even if you don't work in this field you probably have talent working with textured materials, sculpting, or weaving and embroidering. **6** always sees the details and has a very good eye for the harmonizing effect of visuals. This means that *your* taste is also the *public* taste (whereas a **7** may want to push the boundaries of what is new and avant-garde, and would suffer because the market hasn't caught on yet). **6**s make it their business to please the general palate, and provide it with satisfying ingredients.

You may be good with flowers, perfumes, photography and jewellery – trimmings that lift us out of monotony or banality. Businesses connected with these extras will serve you well.

Teaching Teachers are so often **6**s. This is surely because the job demands skill and intelligence married to patience and kindness. **6** brings such varied gifts that those with this number are especially suited to teaching young children: being able to sing and read to young ones, heal their wounds, soothe their disputes, is as important as instructing them. Your number handles all of this with ease.

This list isn't exhaustive – a **6** will bring their strengths to almost any job – but it does offer a taste of what kinds of field will most appeal to your number.

And for luck?

Whatever your work, you will achieve your maximum potential if you use a name to work with that includes the letters F, O or X. Remember this when you are choosing a company name, if you go into business for yourself. It will help, too, for you to optimize your energy and positive attitude, if you decorate your work environment in the scarlet-henna hues of full summer. If you are going for an important interview, these colours would make a positive choice in your outfit, as they help you to project yourself in your most attractive and sensitive light.

WORK PROFILE

The 6 female boss

Exuding a gentle **unhurriedness** in the midst of freneticism, a **6** female boss is wonderfully **in control** of her underlings, yet manages to avoid being a dominatrix. Not averse to using all the gentle arts of her **persuasive** tongue to get someone to agree to sign their weekend away, she **demands loyalty** as her right: she knows she has only to command in the **softest** way, and no one will want to let her down.

The air around her office space will be redolent of her **distinctive scent**, and whatever her taste runs to at the perfumery (she would never buy anything from the airport duty free!), she alone uses it at work, for no one else would dream of trespassing on the signature fragrance that tells passers-by a lady of some **nobility** and **taste** is near. When she joins her partners or peers at a conference meeting, a small space of **calm** surrounds her, and all men gravitate to her – even if they pinch themselves afterwards for **falling for her charms** time and time again.

But don't let this non-aggressive exterior fool you into thinking she's easy in business, with no head for accounts: **6** women at the helm **drive a harder bargain** than the feistiest men! Well aware of their impact on others, and their tools of **beauty** and the power of **gentle speech**, **6**s can talk anyone into anything and still get the best price. You've seen her at work – **imperceptibly goading** her partners and foreign associates into taking risks, with all the calming **reassurance** of Bambi fluttering her lovely long eyelashes. Surely she is never one to take advantage? Just the opposite, because the **6** boss wrong-foots her team and her competitors alike, and gets them to agree to almost inconceivable things. She is one persuasive lady.

WORK PROFILE

The 6 male boss

With an eye for the good-looking members of staff and a sweet but **unforced charm** over all the ladies – especially the older ones – the **6** male boss is a **riddle**. He has a boyishness about him, and a **maturity** in tough circumstances. His personal style is his own: if not traditionally handsome, he has something that distinguishes him. He is **warm**, humorous and **kind**, but **tough** at exacting what he needs to make the business sing along. Underestimate him at your peril, because he **knows what he wants** and doesn't believe in luck. You get what you put into the pot, and any success is entirely derived from effort and follow-through.

A **6** man in charge has **many strings** to his bow – and this may be a problem. It's hard for him to relinquish control – not because he doesn't trust others, but because he wants to be helpful. Still, no one will be more **appreciative** or **generous** in rewarding excellence. Your **6** male boss will take all his protégés out for a fancy lunch – management and groundlings treated equally! The **6** man has **style**.

Most of the company adore him – though some wonder what the fuss is about! His assistant may have a crush on him, but he's unlikely to upset the peaceful atmosphere by mingling office politics and relationships. He loves all the problems brought to him, concerning anything from personnel to postage; a **6** boss of either gender is the office parent, **nurturing** their underlings, but the **6** male is especially interested in **fostering new talent**.

He probably uses a shortened nickname, and enjoys the **lack of formality** on his team. He **demands respect**, though, which should show itself in a thorough acquaintance with the job on the table. More **thorough** than a **3** but less of a stickler than a **4**, this man is almost the **perfect employer**. Lucky team.

WORK PROFILE

The 6 female employee

With an **amenable** air that is absolutely sincere, other employees either loved or loathed her on her first day at work. How can someone be so well-groomed, **on the ball**, not in the least jealous of other people's looks and talents, and **effortlessly at ease** with management as much as the girls in the typing pool? She works the office space **gracefully** and can offer a little bit of help **everywhere** – from knowing how to solve a printing disaster to filling in just the right word for a report, or slipping into a lengthy meeting with freshly brewed coffee without being asked. She makes herself **invaluable** – and quickly.

The **6** girl on the up covers anything she doesn't know with a **willingness to learn**. She was delighted to get the job – though always felt certain she deserved it! – and never loses her sense of how **lucky** she is to be there. She wants to earn well and is prepared to work long hours to make the right impression and show her **dedication**; yet she is never as locked down as a **4** can be, nor as flighty as a **3**. Her **charm** and **personal style** are always going to please, and, though some people won't like her just because she manages to do everything so well, she is only going to be at ground-floor level for a while.

Her **patience** may drive other mortals mad – and other women may feel intimidated by her, and wonder why she is so **nice** to them. It's part of her make-up, but she isn't quite perfect! A quarrel with her boyfriend or a misunderstanding with her mum is likely to give her a long, **gloomy** day, and her personal life does take on enormous importance. She is brilliant at **holding the fort** for others if they are unwell or running late, but at times she's not the world's best timekeeper. She may be late, but she **rarely hurries**. And it's that **calm** that everyone loves.

WORK PROFILE

The 6 male employee

Instantly **appealing** to the females he is working with, the **6** man starting out enjoys all the varied aspects of his job. True, he won't thank you for asking him to carry loads of books upstairs or to clean up after last night's impromptu party, but he is content doing research, writing background or personnel reports, and – especially – illustrating ideas with nifty drawings in the margin. He can **turn his hand** to a surprising number of tasks – and is always more than **willing** to do so.

And his personal style is a topic of conversation. Usually staying fairly **safe** with **conventional** taste, he will throw a cashmere scarf around his neck at the first sign of cool weather, and, if anyone can carry off a pink shirt or accessory, it's him. He wants to make a **personal**

statement, to be noticed; but he never wants his behaviour to be thought crass or vulgar. He wants to be known for what he can *do*.

This easy-going **6** is astonishingly **well-informed** on a number of subjects. He reads and goes to the cinema, so is well up with popular culture and equally able to fill in a missing name or title when it comes up at a conference table. If a colleague is sick, he's **ready** to fill in for them in a moment ... having first made them a cup of tea or sent them home in a taxi. He is comfortable enough working with other men but, let's face it, number **6** is a female number, and – without slurring his masculinity in the slightest – he is really at his best working with or for other women. He is **charming**, but the nice things he says are **sincere**; and he's a **hard worker** when a situation demands his full commitment. Emotional, and always a little worried about others, he is a good **team-worker** who will be ready soon enough to take **responsibility**.

Ideal world or cruel world?

Best and worst jobs ...

IN AN IDEAL WORLD

Best job for a 6 female: Head of a publishing house specializing in arts books (able to exercise excellent taste and people skills, and enjoy keeping up with what's happening in her favourite dominion)

Best job for a 6 male: Film director surrounded by constant flow of creative people and ideas, with a controlling eye over every facet (success brings good money and just enough fame, but still allows family time)

IN A CRUEL WORLD

Worst job for a 6 female: Matron of a mental health-care ward or an old people's home (acute desire to help, but financial constraints and reality of not being able to make enough difference causes distress)

Worst job for a 6 male: Window dresser trapped in a department-store basement (ideas but no showcase for them, no luxury goods to excite the senses; torture!)

6'S CHILDHOOD

Seeing the way a number expresses itself in someone very young is fascinating, for the tendencies and responses are all in their infancy – and yet plain to see. Some facets of a number's power need to be grown into, and take time to reveal how they will be dealt with by the developing character. Sometimes the strength of a number can be a frustration when we're young.

If looking back on your own childhood through the lens of your number, you should discover – with considerable humour and irony – a renewed understanding of some of the difficulties or excitements you experienced. Or, if you have a child who is also a **6**, you may learn something more useful; it is an advantage to understand the qualities a number exudes over an awakening personality, especially in relation to talents and career strengths, as it might save a lot of frustrations. You'll be able to appreciate the positive traits, and handle negative ones more sympathetically.

Here, we take a detailed look at what it's like to be a child bearing your number. But what about the other numbers? Perhaps you have a child who is a **1**, and you'd like to know what that means? Or maybe you'd like to gain insight into friends' and siblings' childhoods, to see if it sheds any light on the people they have become today? A short profile is given for each number, along with advice for a **6** parent on dealing with other-number offspring.

Just as your own parents would have discovered when you were a child, the hardest thing with a **6** child is dealing with their sensitivity and need for affection, keeping them calm and involved in productive, creative tasks. **6**s, as you know, need serenity at all costs, as trauma or argument makes them feel ill, weak or unfocused ...

The young 6

A child born on the 6th, 15th or 24th of any month is a nurturing, gentle and fascinating little person. Think, in fact, of this sensitive child as more of an adult in miniature, a character with a capacity to observe people and things very carefully, and to exercise considerable independence in judgement.

The **6** child will do anything for their family, possessing a deep loyalty to those they love, and has a great deal of maturity about their personal space. This is a child willing to keep their bedroom or play area well-organized purely for the sake of avoiding angry exchanges about it – and also because they need a clear, unfettered space to think and create or read. Peace is vital to a **6** throughout their whole life, and a family constantly battling is the worst kind of exposure a **6** child could have. **6** wants everyone to get on, and any kind of split in the family will have a huge impact on a young **6**. If break-ups do happen between parents, the **6** child at least needs to feel that there is accord and dignity about the arrangements. It is hard to imagine a young **6** siding with either parent against the other one, and it would be cruel to ask them to do so.

Parents carry the responsibility of fostering their **6** child's exceptional talent; if a parent is too self-absorbed to see what they have on their hands, it will truly be a terrible waste. From their youngest years, **6**s have an eye for colour and design – whether they are budding fashionistas who can orchestrate ten items of wardrobe to superb effect, or architects in the making, fascinated by formulating the most restful and aesthetically pleasing use of light and floor space. Any creative tools will interest them, and a box of paints or colouring pencils will be put to inspirational use by any **6** child.

6's toys

Paints • Books • Musical instruments • MP3 player • Craft kits • Cookery books • Mini kitchen utensils and apron • Playhouse • Expensive doll to look after • Pony, or other animals (not strictly 'toys', but an excellent gift for a **6** child, as they will look after them so well)

It may be fair to say that music is the other strong, driving force in a **6**'s life, and this will also make itself evident in the first seven years of childhood. A **6** child sings beautifully, or has the right kind of patience and inner quiet to play the cello; drums might be better kept for a **5** or even a **3**! Give a **6** child their own sound system, and you are unlikely to be blown out of your house by them. Noise is not a **6** failing, and trust will work wonders for a grown-up, kind-hearted **6** child.

As a **6** is always gently entertaining, expect concerts

or little plays when you have guests. **6** is looking for approval but also wants to contribute, and this is not the same kind of performance ethic that will come from the naturally exuberant **6** child or the show-off but sunshiney **5**. A **6** is always thinking about what they are doing, and how others will react.

School and friends have great significance for **6**s, and it is vital to take the time to get these right. A school must become an extended home for a **6**, and gatherings with friends are tremendously important. It's no use having great pals who live miles away and cannot come for a visit regularly. In fact, **6**s take great pains over the friends they make – getting on well with many people – and they work hard to keep them. A **6** child will be the one welcoming the new girl in the class, or taking the boy who has just fallen over to see the school nurse. These friends, made in early life, are likely to remain firm till the end of time, in a **6**'s life.

A young **6** will cook for you on your birthday, make the gift and wrap it exquisitely; on a bad day, they will just provide a hug. This is a gentle and fascinating person who will repay your kindnesses forever. Just make sure you invest enough time in them.

The 1 child

This resourceful child has a different way of thinking, and will stand to one side and evaluate things without pressure. Repeat Grandma's sound advice on any subject to a **1** under the age of six, and they'll simply ask, 'Why?' Ignoring the social expectation to conform, **1** children often make us laugh with surprise.

A **1** child is tough and active – an inquisitive soul who wants to get on with things and not be held in check by others, however wise the parental eye might be. Stubborn and impatient, **1**s frequently suffer by questioning – though not from rudeness – the authority of a parent or teacher. **1**s break down tradition and find new ideas to form a fresh understanding of the world we're in. Your **1** child needs careful handling: a bright mind bursting with interest and disinclined to authority needs subtle direction. If **1** children dominate their friends and talk over their family it can make them socially inept and unable to co-operate in love relationships later in life, leading to loneliness rather than just self-reliance.

A **1**'s greatest challenge is to learn to live in a social world and understand that they are not inevitably right. To foster a **1**'s unique personality and avoid insensitivity to others, let them behave like an adult. This confidence a **1** child will ably repay. **1** children suffer from being misunderstood, as they're often so happy in their private hours and so demanding of having their own time that they may not learn to express their need for others. The seeds are sown early as to how to approach another person for signs of affection, and a loving **6** parent will know perfectly how to 'invade' their **1** child's space without causing alarm, offering gentle hugs at the appropriate moment. But don't cosset your independent **1** too much, or they'll simply try to break free.

The 2 child

All children born on the 2nd or 20th need affection and a peaceful environment to grow up in. Those born on the 11th or 29th are a little different, being master number **11**s with **2** as the denominator, and they have an old head on young shoulders from the beginning of their lives. But even they – for all their drive toward excitement and adventure – will be happiest if their home life is mostly secure and tranquil.

These highly sensitive and intuitive children know what you will say before you say it. They are also dreamy and process ideas in their sleep, waking to instinctive and wise solutions to their problems. But they are vulnerable, and need reassuring more than most numbers. They are acutely sensitive to criticism, feeling that all comments are proof that they're not quite good enough, so you need to deliver your words with tact and an awareness of their needs.

2 children are talented artists, actors, dancers and/or musicians: they know how others *feel*. A **2** child prefers to support friends and family as often as possible, and this can make them a doormat ready to be walked on unless those they live with are alert to their inclinations. If the **2** is an **11**, the wish to help out will be very strong indeed, but these children also have a finely tuned moral sense and will be offended by injustice – especially against them! Don't dish out judgement until you have all the facts.

2s are good healers and can make others feel better. Knowing when to cuddle or touch and when to be quiet, they often have a stillness which works miracles around the sick, the sad and the elderly. A **6** parent will reciprocate and respect this, always ready with affection and praise, appreciating their **2** child's need for inner calm. You will always enjoy the love and support you receive from your gentle, intelligent **2**.

The 3 child

From the cradle, **3**s hold parties and like to mix with other children. They have a capacity to laugh and precipitate laughter, even when things go a little wrong. **3** children are like the reappearing sun after rain, and their energies can be restorative for everyone. Creative and playful, nothing keeps them low for long.

Like a juggler keeping plates and balls in the air, **3**s have several activities and talents on the go from the start. This can be a problem, however: making decisions is hard for them, and they need a wise older counsellor who can talk out the options and give them room to think. Even then, a decision once reached can always be changed – and a **3** child will find a way to run in several directions at one time.

Keep your **3** busy with lots of artistic activities, using colours and textures – right from babyhood – to open their eyes to what they can do. Even before the age of ten a strong personal taste will begin to develop – and it may not be the same as their parents'. Using up their flow of energy on a multitude of tasks will be demanding on both parents, but the **3** child does give a great deal back in return.

3s are talkers and have a witty repartee, even when tiny: you'll be surprised at what you hear from them sometimes, and will wonder where it came from. Naturally gifted at PR, they will talk you around when you are set against one of their wishes, but you will need to direct them now and again or nothing will ever be finished! A **6** parent with a **3** child must give them freedom to experiment, and try not be upset if they are sometimes messy or chatter too much. Be loving and kind, and don't worry if they rush about without your serenity; they have a way of coming back smiling.

The 4 child

Surprisingly insecure and in need of praise, these children are reliable and hard-working and want to do well. They are their own worst critics at times, second only to number **7** children, and they glow when appreciated. They are happiest with family around them – even extended members – and often prefer holidays in familiar places. That said, they can be very quiet and self-sufficient when required, for they concentrate well.

These are organized children who won't cope well if their parents aren't as organized as they are! Never lose a school form or an item from their games kit on a crucial day, as this will cause them serious panic. They like to have material possessions around them because this bolsters their feeling of security, and will manage their pocket money well, content to do odd jobs and chores to gain this reward.

4s love the earth and buildings. They will treasure a patch of garden given them to tend, or a garden house they can extend or build outright. If they are born on the 22nd, rather than the 4th, 13th or 31st, they will truly have architectural talents, and may follow design as a career later. All **4** children, though, are handy at craft work and excellent at projects which require intelligence combined with method to get something done. They hate being late and don't admire tardiness in others, either.

As children, **4**s are loyal and dependable to family and friends, and are more patient than many numbers. They will make light of complex tasks, but need to be allowed to do things their own way. A **6** parent may be proud of their **4** child's care and order, but perhaps think them slightly unimaginative; they simply have a different approach. **4**s feel responsible to others, which you'll encourage, and you respect their tenacity. Your serenity and their focus blend well, and the relationship will grow stronger with time.

The 5 child

Unable to be confined or sit still, a **5** child is bursting with curiosity. Very sociable and happy to be on the move, these adventurous youngsters have much in common with **1**s, but are more willing to work in a team, and good at picking up on other people's ideas, only to improve them.

From their first few words, **5** children have good memories and a facility for speech – they speak and learn quickly, and can pick up more than one language. Even more physical than **1**s (although the two numbers are alike in this), they are excellent at sport or physical co-ordination. They chatter, are full of energy, and like to play to an audience. But most importantly, **5** children love to be free – to explore, laze, hunt, create, discover and travel. Take your **5** child away on holiday and they quickly make friends with others, and acquire a taste for foreign places. They will even experiment with different food, if you're lucky.

5s find a reason to slip away if they're bored with adult company – so don't be offended. Their minds can pursue several streams of active interest, so they need a great deal of amusement to stretch them. This adventurous spirit can be a worry to their family sometimes and, indeed, **5**s need to understand house rules about asking first, or telling someone where they're off to. The difficulty is that **5** children usually don't want to explain themselves to anyone.

The test for a **5**'s parent is to set their child constructive challenges that will vent their curiosity in good ways. **5**s will pick up technology and music (other forms of language, in a sense) quickly, but they don't like dull routine work – which will irritate a **4** sibling if they have one. A **6** parent of a **5** child will need to give them more freedom to do their own thing, and will hate their restlessness and noise but admire their imaginative talents and creativity. You will need to be patient, though!

The 7 child

Even in primary school this is a child with a focused mind and a strongly developed critical sense. A **7** child is perceptive and, sometimes, disarmingly quiet. They will often prefer adult company, as their peers will probably seem too young and underdeveloped to them. Wise and difficult to know well, these are children with a serious cast to their intelligent minds.

The fact that a **7** child can sit quietly and contemplate things deeply should not imply that they are introverted: quite the opposite. A **7** will grow into a very good host as long as the company appeals, and they have a lovely sense of humour, apparent from their earliest years – even if it does sometimes find expression at others' expense. They will rarely be rude, but certainly have a good understanding of all that has been said – and what has not been.

Listen to their impressions of the people they deal with!

All **7**s as children have an inward reluctance to accept other people's ideas automatically – rather like **1**s – but there is a special propensity to independence in a child born on the 16th. This is the number of someone who finds it difficult asking for what they want – someone who often feels as though they haven't been consulted as to their own wishes. And all **7**s certainly have definite ideas about what to believe.

7 children should be told the truth on virtually all matters; they will know if they are being deceived, and will respect being treated as an adult in any case – which is easy for a **6** parent. Even you may find their maturity unnerving, but you will respect your **7** child's strength and drive to excel in what they like. Though different, your numbers appreciate each other, and a **7** child gives any parent much to be proud of, both academically and in terms of humanitarian feelings.

The 8 child

Here we have a young executive in the making. Even when they are still at school these children have a canny nose for what will make good business – and yet they are generous, hard-working and prepared to learn everything it will take to succeed in this life. Children born on the 8th, 17th and 26th like to have charge of their own finances, and to be given scope to do 'grown-up' activities – organizing their own parties and making arrangements for outings with their friends.

These children have strength and energy, but mentally are reflective and wise, too. They always see both sides to an argument – so parents who ask them to choose sides, beware! An **8** makes good judgements, and even before the age of ten they have a sense of what is fair and what is morally right.

As this number rules the octave, many **8** children are extremely musical and have a wonderful sense of rhythm. This last even assures they can be good at sport, as it takes innate timing to perfect many physical skills. **8**s also like philosophical ideas and relish being given 'big concepts' to chew over, especially concerning politics or religious ideas. **8**s are proud, and like to research things carefully – so as long as they are not bored, you will find an **8** child with their head in a book or on the internet, or watching programmes that educate and broaden their vistas.

An **8** child is always striving for balance, like you, though you must be pragmatic if they are sometimes pulling in the opposite direction from you. Though they are independent, they are loyal to those they love, and have a delicate sensibility that makes them look at the other side of a story, or fight for an underdog. As a **6**, you understand this care of others very well, and (mostly) you will respect the qualities and mind of your generous, driven **8**.

The 9 child

Here is a person born for the theatre, or to travel the world and befriend everyone. **9**s have an expansive view of things, and don't like to be restricted. With a good head for both science and the arts, there are many career directions a **9** may take, so parents will have their work cut out trying to help them choose. However, because the number **9** is like a mirror, with every number added to it reducing again to that same number (for example: 5+9 = 14, and 1+4 = 5), **9** children are able to take on the feelings of just about anyone, which is why they are so artistic and good at drama and writing.

From their first years in school it will be clear a **9** child has a wonderful dry sense of humour and a taste for the unusual. **9** children are not often prejudiced and seem to be easy-going – though they are sensitive to the atmosphere around them, picking up vibes like a sponge. If you speak to them harshly they will take it seriously, and are protective of others who seem to be hurt in this way too.

9s have a delicate relationship with their parents, but particularly with the father figure. A **9** girl will want to idolize her dad, and will feel desperately disappointed if circumstances are against this, while a **9** boy may wish to emulate his father – and yet they often grow up without enough input from this important person, who is busy or away. A **9** child must be wise ahead of their time, and so this lesson is thrown at them in one guise or another.

The **6** parent of a **9** child understands how to be hospitable, allowing a stream of friends and interests through the door. Your **9** child appreciates your warmth, and recognizes your pride in them, rewarding you with affection and kindness. Grown-ups from the start, their philosophical mind and willingness to keep the peace fill you with admiration – but don't hold them too tight!

6 AT PLAY

We have discovered how your number expresses itself through your character in relation to your family and your general personality, what instinctive reactions go with your number in everyday situations, and how it might shape your career path and colour your childhood. But every day our DAY number also influences the way we respond to the social world around us. So, what can it say about our leisure hours? Is yours a number that even allows itself to relax? (Well, you probably already have some answers to this one!) What can your number reveal about the way you like to spend your time, or how you achieve pleasure outside of duty?

Over the next few pages we take a look at what makes you tick, as a **6**, when you are unwinding – and how **6**s prefer to fill their time, if given a choice. Let's see whether you're typical in this respect ... And who knows – if you haven't already tried all the activities and pastimes mentioned, maybe you'll get a few ideas about what to put on your list for next time!

The 6 woman at play

Looking back over the main traits of a **6**'s character, you will notice a recurring theme of needing to be creative as an individual but also requiring vital recuperation time and quiet. In your leisure hours, these needs – often quite diverse – are likely to be equally fed, and certainly you will want to balance the desire for socializing with dear friends and lovers alongside the longing for serenity and calming thinking time. Usually, you manage to fit in both.

There's nothing wrong with admitting that you (and **6** men too) can be a sybarite! You are the most generous hostess, and love to have an extended family of friends and relatives around to eat or stay on a regular basis. And it is not uncommon for a **6** to plan their weekend off playing host to others, arranging every detail to perfection, tying fresh flowers into pretty bunches and choosing beautiful soap and linen for guests who are sleeping over. **6**s always take care of such details: your home will be the closest to a luxury bed and breakfast that your space can afford.

But this level of cosseting is also strongly appealing to you: a spa weekend was designed for a **6** and her girlfriends, and every exquisite touch, from the beautiful towels to the gentle music and feeling of peace, is exactly the sort of thing to make a **6** girl smile. This would even be an ideal honeymoon or pamper break with a lover: 'his and hers' robes and slippers, and a few quiet hours to enjoy the atmosphere and then just indulge in conversation. Romantic and restorative: love and peace – bywords for a **6**.

And, in fact, *romance* is part of your leisure time. Whether getting a new relationship off the ground with stylish, seductive plans or rejuvenating a long-term tie, you take the greatest pleasure in spending time spoiling your partner. Any tranquil pursuits shared together are as good as a week off for a **6**: strolling beside watery harbours and dipping in and out of charming eateries, a **6** counts love and eating as a hobby. Though not as physically restless as a **5** or as frantic about *doing* as a **3**, you will enjoy gentle time spent cycling through the countryside with family, or walking in the hills with your man. Keeping on the move just a little is a sign of sociability – as long as the movement is not frenzied and allows time for thought and exploration of your co-traveller's mind.

Hours spent at an easel, or making jam, are hobby hours for a **6**, and shopping is true therapy when you need a quick tonic after a bustling week. If your children are in tow, they are going to be as spoiled by your credit card as you are, because **6** loves spending money on others too. But if your inner signalling station is switched to its more 'spiritual' or 'meditative' gear, a course in sketching or art history will appeal. Actually, **6**s adore history, and sniffing out long-forgotten corners in old towns or snooping delightedly in antiques shops will create hours of fascination on an away-day. And this extends to your reading list: **6**s love a good book for a (blissfully!) quiet evening, and historical novels or books about the past are a must-have on your beautifully finished shelves. There's always a novel in your gorgeous overnight bag: it allows others around you some space too, and they appreciate it.

As for where to draw the line at what will amuse a **6** in her leisure pursuits, this can be tricky. Everything artistic has a magnetic attraction: you're as comfortable at the opera as at the theatre, and can flick a mood switch to get into role for a pop concert – especially if a loved one wants to go too. If the day is sunny and the scene pretty enough, you'll give many things a try, from packing an epicurean picnic to berrying with a beautiful pannier, or from painting the lighthouse on the point to hunting for a historical house or botanical garden. And, if the rain has settled in, you'll be baking or reading, with the ever-present music in the background. A **6**'s leisure? You exude it in all you do!

The 6 man at play

You are happiest whiling away your leisure hours to make someone else happy. You know it's true! If a loved one asks for a fresh coat of paint in the bathroom or a new shelf for books, the obliging and diversely talented **6** male will use his weekend to achieve it. Always happy to add new creative tricks to your repertoire, you are adept at home decorating, tiling, painting and gardening, and you could even sculpt a garden feature at a push. More impressively, these activities count as pleasure hours for you.

But you know how to relax, as well. Films may well be a must for you, as you love to watch a complete visual presentation done by someone with talent. Browsing a gallery, catching an exhibition, fitting in a concert – all of these art-related pleasures jostle for a **6** man's leisure time. You probably work hard and need a break, too, because **6** men are generally anxious to provide little luxuries for their families. But even if it's a rare weekend off, you will help in the kitchen – if not take centre-stage there – when your mother-in-law is visiting, or when a friend with a problem drops in for a chat. You are used to being the good host and wise friend.

Travel is important for a **6** man, but whereas a **1** looks for new territory each time, and a **5** picks somewhere with hustle and bustle, *you* will return over and over to the places you fell in love with years ago. Besides, you met people there, and they remain friends forever. You know the romantic spots in the backstreets of New York, Paris and Rome – and even the outback of Australia, if you're given the chance to show your partner. This is largely because of your love of solitude and peace; you're an expert at digging out those quiet corners in noisy places, where a soul can think. Your taste certainly runs to the quiet, established hotels where flashiness is outlawed and subtlety is required – and probably, with a little luck, your budget also runs to it.

A **6** man likes to educate himself in his free time. You will read a good paper from cover to cover, including the supplements – if there is no time for more; otherwise, we can expect to see you surfing the net for information on what you don't know. If you can manage a week away without thinking of others' needs simultaneously, you love to pursue some form of adult education. This is not because of mental restlessness – which a **5** might feel – or the striving for greater knowledge and perfection that besets a **7**; a **6** is inspired to know more for the sake of unhurried and accurate thought. It is part of your *pleasure* to understand.

Surprisingly sporty – partly because you have good rhythm – you probably swim, run or dance well, sing semi-professionally, or take excellent photographs. You like to do any and all of this on your days away, and these talents are likely to remain on an amateur level, because you're not compelled to be the best, or a perfectionist, as a **7** would be. You are more like Lorenzo de' Medici – the fifteenth-century Italian statesman, poet and scholar who was a highly gifted dilettante – and this is endearing, making others feel you are more relaxed, and not off-puttingly competitive. And, although comment on your love life properly belongs in the following section (*see overleaf*), it is as well to say here that whoever loves you need not be jealous. You have lots of lady friends, because you like and respect women. Your partner needs to hold you gently – but must hold you. You need love, a little calm and quiet, and a pretty space to live in ...

6 IN LOVE

Love: it's what we all want to know about. What's your style as a lover? And your taste – where does that run? Do you want a partner who is, ideally, as affable and as socially generous as you? Or would it suit you better to have a quieter partner who is steady and solid, and who lets you do the entertaining? Everything about you says 'hospitality', but is a co-host all you need to find in order to have a happy love life?

Our first task is to consider how you see others as potential partners, and what you are likely to need from them. Why are you attracted to someone in the first place? This is where we begin ... But then you might like to pass the book across to your other half (if you have one), for the second subject of discussion is: why are *they* attracted to *you*? What does it mean to have a **6** lover?

Telltale traits of the 6 lover

- Affectionate, warm, keen to please
- Usually easy-going
- Responds to a creative or charismatic lover, as 6 likes to follow a little at times
- Needs a partner who can accommodate family cares and wants to co-create a home
- Sometimes a little smothering
- Very loving and peaceable

How do you do?
A **6** IN ATTRACTION

All **6**s love company, so meeting people is never a problem for this social-bunny number. You are a good host yourself, and love to accept invitations, so your party personality certainly gets a regular enough airing! But who will catch your eye, and what are you looking for in love?

Strangely enough, **6**s rarely become attracted to anyone whose speaking voice they don't love the sound of. Every number will take a good-looking partner if they can get one, but it is almost unique to **6** alone that the way someone sounds – in addition to the way they express themselves – is a crucial part of the magnetism. You are genuinely arrested if you hear someone speaking in a striking way, and for this reason you may find yourself drawn over and over again to a lover who is a musician or an actor, or someone used to public speaking. The commanding sound of another human being is quite an aphrodisiac for sensual **6**. And if anyone flirts with you over a keyboard, playing you a little Chopin, or reveals some expertise with those sexy Spanish guitar strings, you're putty in their hands.

Off the beaten track

You have very developed taste visually, and it is true of **6**s that they will often appreciate beauty or exciting looks in someone whom others might consider a little offbeat or out of fashion. A **6** man will be drawn to a woman whose looks might span several ages, and he will determine very quickly whether she will improve with age, like a good wine. This is intoxicating to him. Similarly, a **6** woman is unafraid to go for a partner who is not considered the norm – rather than someone whom everyone agrees is handsome or conventionally attractive.

This really is because **6** looks deeper than the skin, and sees past fashion. You have an excellent visual perception, brokered by a spiritual feeling. Someone having wonderful eyes, for instance, may be the single most important factor in physical attraction for you – and this is not least because **6**s always seem to have very beautiful or dazzling eyes themselves, too. For every **6**, the eyes are the window to the soul, and an unusual colour or intensity speaks of depth of human feeling and sense. Very beguiling for you!

You are probably not attracted by anyone who is brash or vulgar in any case, but there is one factor that is simply not open for debate: your beloved must have style and a generosity of spirit. A **6** cannot form a relationship with someone who is mean or constrained – either financially or emotionally. Being naturally generous yourself, you want to make gestures of affection that dip into your pocket, and if the person you are developing feelings for doesn't respond well, you will cool off. And you also expect (and will usually receive) little material signs of admiration from a loved one, as well.

6s don't hold their feelings in very well and, though they may be keen on serenity and avoiding emotional love-storms, it is a number that hates playing around – and hates others doing it too!

A sucker for romance

You will enjoy a partner you feel safe with, for **6** needs a little demonstrative behaviour from its lovers. It may sound old-fashioned, but the one who will woo you is the one who surprises you with gestures like flowers, and novel ways of getting a text or e-mail to you when you least expect it. **6**s attract many interested parties, being attractive and warm-hearted, but they will only give their heart to someone who has romantic style. The grand gesture is important for you, and this is, in part, due to the way it makes you feel securely loved and – potentially – signals that there will be financial security in the future.

Once you have agreed to date the person with the distinctive voice and interesting (possibly slightly recherché?) fashion style, you will quietly begin an analysis of how much you have in common to interest you over time. Other numbers (notably **1**, **3** and **5**) love a challenge in a relationship, and a **7** will unwittingly look for dramas in personal ties; but **6** is not a number that wants trouble in the days ahead. To avoid disappointment, a little quiz might appear over the starter course on a first date: favourite film, best-loved city, contents of the CD collection ... A **6** likes to know these little details – and finds it uncannily revealing.

Not to say that you don't love to convince someone out of the ordinary of your own 'out-of-the-ordinariness', you do, nevertheless, want a bond with a person who can fit into your very aesthetic and soothing world. This must be someone who is a willing partner for a trip to a gallery or a restaurant, or even a Saturday night out on the tiles, and someone who will notice (and appreciate) the trouble you've taken to put crisp, fresh linen on the bed, and to offer luxury soap in the bath. Someone who's a mean economizer will be offered the door after just a single weekend!

All you want is ...

So what do you want, as a **6**, in a love affair? That's easy: an interesting person with diverse talents (important), who loves your cooking and cooks a little too; someone who has a kind heart towards others, and is aware of what is going on in the world that shouldn't be; and a person who wants to support you while you make little changes to the worlds' ills. Oh, and it should be someone with taste who loves music – because **6** is only half a person if they live without it – who has no fear of making a commitment, and who wants to shower you in little tokens of true love. And if they can love your family – and that includes tolerating Great-Uncle George, who repeats everything three times and talks very loudly – this is probably your perfect love!

To have and to hold?

LOVING A NUMBER 6

If you have fallen for a **6**, there's a crucial factor that you need to understand from the outset: you'd better get used to doing things in a **6**'s way. Of course you are attracted to a beautiful **6** – why wouldn't you be? They are so well turned out, everything finished to the last detail, conscious of making things comfortable in the living room and in the kitchen, with almost imperceptible attention to others' feelings at all times ...

This is an intuitive, romantic, sensitive soul who seems like no other person you've met. Loving a **6** is an obvious thing to do – with their multi-talents in seamless directions, and their effortless but gentle social skills. A **6** demands that you are intrigued by them, because there never seems to be a limit to what they can do or where they might go, and it all appears to happen around them magically. No one sees the effort a **6** puts into life, and it is a fascinating sleight-of-hand trick watching a **6** succeed on the social stage.

What a wonderful world

You may be amused by the number of different people your **6** knows, because they get on with so many. It could be that you even met through some very strange branch of mutual connections: a **6** likes swimming as an enjoyable exercise, and collects the people who swim at the same pool as friends; or knows the owner of their favourite restaurant by name, and remembers all the waiters and waitresses; or went backstage after a pop concert, because they have a friend in the band ... In every odd place, **6** knows someone. Every one of these roads is a fascinating revelation, and you will certainly look forward to some weird and wonderful extended relationships if you are dating a **6**.

And then there's sex. We haven't yet mentioned a **6**'s mighty pulling power over others physically. They may not be the most handsome or beautiful, the most physically fit, or the best-dressed person in the crowd, but **6** exudes such enigmatic, quiet sexiness that you simply *have* to know more ...

A **6** is never as outré about a physical appetite or conquest as a **3** or a **5**, nor as obviously libidinous; yet they are simply sexually desirable, and give the signal to interested parties that love with them will be an experience – sensual and pleasurable, and yet nicely private. If it's true that life in bed with a **3** would be full of laughter, and with a **5** full of high-octane variety, sharing a bed with a **6** is an unhurried pleasure, and offers a realm of possibility. And this is extremely fetching!

Patience is a virtue

You have to recognize that your **6** love will have other responsibilities. These could run to anything from a demanding parent who needs regular input with regard to a child from a previous relationship (and who may be there at awkward moments), to a past lover who has never quite gone it alone since the break, demanding that kind-hearted **6** still has a role to play. This drinks up patience if you're in love with a **6**; but open contests won't work, and you'd be more likely to lose your lover. **6**s don't make choices with any delight, so whatever there is in the closet you'll probably just have to live with it.

You also need to understand that your **6** is a wonderful person but, nevertheless, both demanding of lovers and idealizing of many relationships. And dramatic confrontations will cause them to retreat. Your **6** will look for peace first and last – sometimes at any price – so bold acts are a dangerous habit to cultivate. Simply give your **6** room to breathe and dream, and be loved, and to have those around them who seem important. A **6** wants bathing in wonderful smells and delicious sounds, and lots of gentle love. The rewards are probably worth the few adjustments, and, if the relationship progresses beyond the first year, the bond is likely to grow and improve with time.

6 in love

Turn-ons:

- ♥ ✔ A lover who allows peace to rule
- ♥ ✔ Someone whose scent and voice are enticing
- ♥ ✔ An appreciative, positive person whose glass is half-full, and who can share your love of the good life
- ♥ ✔ Someone who is similarly creative

Turn-offs:

- ♥ ✗ A disloyal game-player, who is either mean with money or unresponsive to trouble and effort taken on their behalf
- ♥ ✗ A lover who demands dramatic and ostentatious gestures
- ♥ ✗ Someone who is always forcing things too hard and too fast
- ♥ ✗ A person who is too controlling

6'S COMPATIBILITY

In this weighty section you have the tools to find out how well you click with all the other numbers in matters of the heart, but also when you have to work or play together too. Each category opens with a star-ratings chart, showing you – at a glance – whether you're going to encounter plain sailing or stormy waters in any given relationship. First up is love: if your number matches up especially well with the person you're with, you will appreciate why certain facets of your bond just seem to slot together easily.

But, of course, we're not always attracted to the people who make the easiest relationships for us, and if you find that the one you love rates only one or two stars, don't give in! Challenges are often the 'meat' of a love affair – and all difficulties are somewhat soothed if you both share a birthday number in common, even if that number is derived from the *total* of the birth date rather than the actual **DAY** number. In other words, if your partner's **LIFE** number is the same as your **DAY** number, you will feel a pull towards each other which is very strong, even if the **DAY** numbers taken together have some wrinkles in their match-up. You will read more about this in the pages that follow the star chart.

The charts also include the master numbers **11** and **22**: these bring an extra dimension to relationships for those whose birth-number calculations feature either of these numbers at any stage. (For example, someone with a **DAY** number of **2** may be born on the 29th: 2+9 = **11**, and 1+1 = **2**. This means you should read the compatibility pairings for your number with both a **2** and an **11**.)

Sometimes the tensions that come to the surface in

love relationships are excellent for business relationships instead: the competitiveness that can undermine personal ties can accelerate effectiveness in working situations. We'll take a look at how other numbers match up with yours in vocational situations. And, when it comes to friends, you'll see why not all of your friendships are necessarily a smooth ride ...

In all matters – whether love, work or friendship – you will probably discover that the best partnerships you make involve an overlap of at least one number that you share in common. A number **6** attracts other number **6**s in various close ties throughout life.

NOTE: To satisfy your curiosity, **ALL** numbers are included in the star charts, so that you can check the compatibility ratings between your friends, co-workers and loved ones – and see why some relationships may be more turbulent than others!

Love

YOUR **LOVE** COMPATIBILITY CHART

	1	2	3	4	5
With a 1	★★★★	★★★★★	★★	★★★	★★★★★
With a 2	★★★★★	★★★★	★★★	★★★★★	★
With a 3	★★	★★★	★★★★★	★★	★★★★
With a 4	★★★	★★★★★	★★	★★★★	★★
With a 5	★★★★★	★	★★★★	★★	★★★
With a 6	★★★	★★★★	★★★★	★★★	★★
With a 7	★★★★★	★★	★★★	★★★★★	★★★
With an 8	★★★★	★★★★	★★★★★	★★★	★★★
With a 9	★★★	★★★	★★★★★	★★	★★★
With an 11	★★★★	★★★★	★★	★★★★★	★★
With a 22	★★★★	★★★★★	★★★	★★★★	★★★★

6	7	8	9	11	22
★★★	★★★★★	★★★★	★★★	★★★★	★★★★
★★★★	★★	★★★★	★★★	★★★★	★★★★★
★★★★	★★★	★★★★★	★★★★★	★★	★★★
★★★	★★★★★	★★★	★★	★★★★★	★★★★
★★	★★★	★★★	★★★	★★	★★★★
★★★★★	★	★★★	★★★★★	★★★★	★★★★
★	★★★	★★★★	★★★	★★★★	★★★★★
★★★	★★★★	★★★	★★	★★★★★	★★★★
★★★★★	★★★	★★	★★★	★★★★	★★★
★★★★	★★★★	★★★★★	★★★★	★★	★★★★★
★★★★	★★★★★	★★★★	★★★	★★★★★	★★

6 in love with a 1 ★★★

Oops! This is going to be interesting. You have a relationship that works as an attraction of opposites, in many ways, with **6** enticing **1** to slow down and take things carefully, rather than rush off and try to do everything all at once. This is out of care for your **1**, rather than from an over-cautious nature, though it won't always seem so to the **1**. However, if anyone can get independent **1** to admit they need a hug sometimes, maybe you can. **6** is the number of love, and you are a soul wanting to be loved above all else. Result: you will force your **1** to feel their emotions, ask them for a kiss, and tell them when they are being impossible – but ever so gently! No one else can quite manage this with a **1**.

If the **1** is too self-occupied, you will languish. Every personal pain and hurt a **6** feels is related to being loved and needed, whereas a **1**'s wishes are to be left alone to work things through on their own. You are not emotionally weak, but are made strong by love, so the **1** needs to be as expressive as possible if they really love you, and want to make things work over time. Private **1** will also need to get on with your family – to be prepared to have an extended group of people in your shared life. Or, if you don't have that many family members, this could be a source of some pain to you, which a sometimes unthinking **1** will need to bear in mind.

1 loves your good taste, and will learn from it. You can get no-nonsense **1** to look at the world in a different light, and you may also just about persuade this loner to be more sociable and outgoing than they are inclined to be. What you love is the way **1** shines for you and for others, and, if they don't abuse this power, they can be very exciting for you, and open your horizons. However, the seesaw begins to tip the other way if the **1** insists on always seeing things only from their own perspective, and ignoring gentle **6**'s feelings. Sharing creative tastes and projects will probably be the best way to appreciate each other's artistic streak and allow yourselves to be individuals sharing time and space together, with a dash of solitude.

Clashes will happen. They may centre around **1** feeling that you are over-protective of other people in your lives; or, it may be that you seem to smother your **1** occasionally, without letting them have their own room or friends. Not everything between you will be shared, and your tendency to be self-sacrificing may bother the more aggressive **1**, or even make them angry. Once **1**'s respect is lost it is hard to regain. But most of the adjustments must come from them, and it will be imperative that they somehow fight the urge to be dictatorial or pushy, just because you seem to take longer than they do to decide on an important direction to take, or to complete a task.

1 may fall off the pedestal you want to put them on.

So high are your ideals of others that it is sometimes unrealistic to expect anyone to live up to them, but be sensible in how you come to this realization.

Key themes

Share pride in children and family, if they go on to have one • **6** has an urge for luxury, and wants a beautiful place to live • **1** excites **6**'s pride in them, but has to give in to much socializing

6 in love with a 2 ★★★★

This is an excellent romance, with a very good chance of going the distance if you get through the first few months. Your numbers have so many qualities that are akin – from a love of people, entertaining and nurturing to an appreciation of what is beautiful and serene. **2** loves the good life nearly as much as you do, and you will create a relationship of shared interests. Travel appeals, and among many arts and creative enjoyments you are both music lovers, and have a strong magnetic pull toward visual arts. In fact, keeping company together, this relationship could strengthen your individual artistic abilities as a result of the encouragement and appreciation you get from one another.

Neither of you is aggressive, which is a positive – although things may occasionally be too tranquil, with a chance that the relationship could become predictable and complacent. One of you will need to think about the future, and, at various times, either one of you may take the lead in this. **6** is often happy to let **2** dictate the terms, but you will probably feel everything can be a jointly reached decision, and this should work fairly well for both of you. Nor is it a surprise to find **6** and **2** together. Your **2** is drawn at once to your attractive, easy way with people and your skill in the kitchen. And your wonderful eye for the decorative elements of life – fashion and home – will endorse **2**'s own wish to take proper care of how things look around *you*. Affection and tactility will also have a proper place in your love lives, for **6** is sensuous (if a fraction shy, perhaps) in just the same ways as the **2**.

2's developed sense of tact and charm is a huge help to you, as you'll feed off the confidence invested in you both by friends, family and business partners. You are also likely to be very kind to each other about your extended families, with you taking real trouble to know how to please anxious **2**'s relatives and friends – a favour **2** will return. Or, if you don't have a big family (which may be a source of some regret), your sensitive **2** is more than able to fill in the gaps and make a family of just two.

In this, and in many other ways, you are co-operative and considerate of each other's feelings, hurts and highs. **2** also knows how to help you up the ladder work-wise, with gentle pressure and insistence; **6**s often languish without a nudge, and, though you are attractive, kind and fascinating, you are often surprisingly inept at capitalizing on your talents. This is something your **2** will offset with gritty determination, for they understand how to bring the right people around you, to help you along. You are both healers, helpers, teachers, intuitive thinkers who will make time for a life of kindness and service to others. And, blissfully, it is unlikely you'll take advantage of each other in any selfish way. Even if the **2** is an **11**, it's a bond of destiny and higher thinking.

Clashes will happen only when one (or both) of you is

negative about relationships generally. If experience from the past has made either of you guarded, you may drive each other mad with impossible, idealistic demands which have little hope of materializing into a happy reality. You can both be dreamers, and if neither of you gets down to the business of life that is hard work, application and realism – or you allow yourselves to be walked on – the luminous potential of this relationship may meander into misfortune and sadness. However, with so many things in common, this is one of the happiest number-pairings you could wish for. Grab that lovely **2** and walk right into their heart for keeps – for you can hardly do better!

Key themes

Share excellent taste and a wish to beautify their world together • Friends, relatives and children take priority • Lucky financially • A magnetic, attractive couple

6 in love with a 3 ★★★★

There are many good prospects for happiness here, where two naturally creative people full of kindness can make each other very happy. **6** has the substance to help **3** find an outlet for their artistic ability, and **3** draws the sometimes over-serious **6** into more laughter and joy in life. **3**, in fact, may help **6** to be more at ease with the idea of putting their own interests to the fore, as **6** so often retires into a feeling of what is duty. Also a problem is **6** thinking things through too much in life, and not putting their considerable talents behind a dream – but buoyant, energetic **3** will help remedy this. **3** and **6** marry congeniality and a love of people with a flair for synthesizing what is beautiful. This should appeal to both parties.

3 loves your grace and elegance (which is sometimes a character trait as much as a style), and you are always appreciative of **3**'s ease and sociability. Together these numbers find harmony in myriad ways: similar tastes in music and the arts, a willingness to support each other through personal goals, a feeling of pleasure in shared pledges towards friends and family. You, perhaps, even have the advantage of keeping **3** calmer (if anyone can!), while **3** can excite you into action when you might well prefer to sit back and let others steal your thunder. If you are afraid to self-promote, a **3** in love with you will happily do it for you.

A **3** may become a shade less aggressive in company with you. That aggression so often stems from nervous energy and insecurity about their emotions, but you offer **3** more inner tranquillity. Also, gentle **6** may help flighty **3** to think about the future more, and ask them where they want to be a few years from now, helping them to plan and make the most of their exceptional talents. **3** is so used to being capable of so many things, yet failing to capitalize, and you will not only see their potential but glow with pride over their unique star qualities, making them more aware of what they have going for them. Life gets better for oft nervy **3** when someone has true faith in them, which you, sensitively, do.

Meanwhile, **3**'s powerful optimism helps make you believe more in the potential of life. A **6** in love is always happier, because your number needs an outlet for its natural affections, but sometimes you feel life throws burdens and responsibilities at us all to a greater extent than pleasures. **3**, though, has the knack of turning this pessimism away. Reminding you of all that is beautiful in life, **3** helps you to loosen up with others and laugh – and the sound of a **6** laughing is magical! This sense of being needed may deepen the bonds between you. As a **6**, you are always worrying about that apocryphal 'rainy day', and this helps the often scatty **3** to organize their money and accumulate more than usual. You'll gently chide them whenever their wastefulness threatens to become too detrimental.

And what about your love style together? You demand – and get – **3**'s loyalty more than anyone can, keeping them on track for romance. Such a natural flirt, **3** usually gives others the impression that they can't settle. With you, though, they'll want to make a beautiful nest and look after you. Gender becomes irrelevant, and, even if you are older than the **3**, they will make you feel young, confident and desirable ... all of which means this relationship could go the distance, and make you both very happy for many, many years.

Key themes

Each of you wants company • Both fond of pleasure, and enjoy the same kinds of hobby • **6** gives **3** confidence, and **3** makes **6** laugh • The good feeling you generate brings financial luck

6 in love with a 4 ★★★

Even though quite dissimilar, both numbers are relatively gentle and non-aggressive – **6** especially. Consequently, any of the friction that is bound to occur is likely to be dealt with gently, and the relationship may flourish more than one might expect. Both are stubborn, it's true, but beyond a digging-in of heels occasionally, the dynamic between a **6** and **4** offers room for happiness. You are drawn to each other partly as opposites, but this pairing has a good chance of resolving into harmony.

Each offers the other a chance to expand their individual awareness. **4** understands **6**'s craving for affection and security – related somewhat to their own. No one may be better able to supply you with this feeling of being beloved than a **4**. And you instinctively sense when to go softly-softly, every time the **4** is under pressure. You both recognize the importance of concentrated effort to achieve a goal. You have such a vast supply of raw, creative talent, but not always the stamina or self-confidence to bring that to a fruitful end product. **4** understands this, and shores up that lack by keeping your feet firmly on the ground, their eyes on the end prize. These two energies blended offer each other a lot of support and love, and it works well.

But what drew you to each other in the beginning? Why do you feel a magnetic pull towards **4**? Partly, it's because **4** offers that reliable partnership you need to thrive. **6** is the number of love, and its childhood dreams and romantic ideals live or die on how cherished it feels. Without love, a **6** cannot fulfil its potential – which is considerable. Beauty and the arts, and a feeling for others, are part of your nature, but all that you have to offer is contingent on feeling that one other person cares, and that you have someone to care for. **4**'s feet are planted strongly on the ground, and this has a decided appeal.

6's essence is, perhaps, feminine in the sense of being fluid, emotive, intuitive, aesthetic; **4**'s essence is more masculine, being practical and careful, forming ideas on reason. These combine very well – though it is interesting if the **6** is the male and the **4** the female! Either way, **4** is likely to play the anchor, and you will entice them to try out philosophies and venture into fields they may never have gone into alone. **6** softens **4**'s resolute behaviour, while **4** steadies **6**'s anxieties.

4 would have to be cloth-eared and blind not to be aware of your considerable physical and sensual charms, so the attraction will be strong. **6** loves to have a partner – someone who will be on time even when the rain is pouring and the traffic impossible; and that is **4**. Home will be a focus – making a beautiful place to live in, first as a couple, and then with a family. Children will become a priority, and both numbers are proud parents.

You will encourage **4** to loosen those purse strings and splash out for a few of life's material luxuries, and no one is more willing to work hard for such gains. Roughly put, **4** is the builder and **6** the decorator – and this should be a partnership that can create an atmosphere of true happiness and joy. Yes, both partners have their moody days, and refuse to budge on personal views. But there should be more than enough incentive to cope with those days, and, overall, this pairing offers an excellent chance of going the distance, if it can just negotiate the early months where adjustments need to be made.

Key themes

Mutual goals and a need for emotional security • **6** broadens **4**'s outlook, and **4** makes **6** feel secure • Good relationship for material advantages • May prefer life in a more rural environment

6 in love with a 5 ★★

Opposites attract, and that can be a good thing – especially in this partnership, if you are willing to learn from the particular differences that each of you exhibit. **5**s are freewheeling, unconventional lovers, ardent, sensuous and quite demanding, where loving is concerned. Without disturbing your sensibilities here, you bear the number of love, appreciation, nurture and friendship, and as such may find your magnetic **5** entirely too rambunctious, once the initial phase of fascination and intrigue wears off.

If anything, it's the **5** who should make every effort to get to know you well, because if they do they will find that you share some creativity, a love of the arts, and a passion for the finer things in life – good food, creature comforts, firm friends and acquaintances. You have the ability to add finesse to **5**'s undisciplined appreciation, and fine-tune their skills. **5** will value your excellent taste, easy good humour and manner, superb culinary skills – and will learn from all of it. A **6** can get a **5** to slow down for a moment, to look at the world in a different light; and you may also just about persuade **5** to be more considerate and balanced in giving and receiving love and affection.

This is, of course, at best, because a **6** is a soul wanting to be loved above all else. You will force your **5** to *feel* their emotions, ask them for a kiss, and tell them when they are being selfish or impossible – ever so gently.

If **5** is indiscriminate, self-indulgent or capricious, you will pine and fret. A **6**'s pain and hurt is related to needing love, whereas a **5**'s wishes are to be free to do as they please with whom they so desire. You are not spineless, but made stronger by love. **5** will have to be as sincere, sharing and expressive as possible, if they care for your tender heart and want to make the relationship work over time. And what you will love about your **5** is the way in which they sparkle (both for you and for others), their humour and daring, their complete disrespect for inherited ideas and institutions. This is not at all like you, but you may be in awe of **5** for being the rule-breaker, and, if your **5** doesn't abuse this power to speak out, they can be very exciting for a **6**, and open your horizons.

But most of the adjustments must come from you – is this too much to ask? – and it will be imperative that the **5** curbs their natural impulse to be impatient, unaccountable, unreliable and unrestrained just because you want assurances of love and devotion, or because you take your own sweet time to make important choices – a problem that impatient **1** will also feel with you. **5** may then fall from grace in your eyes: so high are the ideals you are looking for in others that it is sometimes unrealistic to expect anyone – especially a **5** – to live up to such a standard. And a **5** may not be the most sensitive person to help you realize that you're after the impossible ...

Key themes

5 excites **6**'s pride in them • **5**s must expect invasions of privacy from friends, old school mates and overseas visitors • Magnetic sexual and creative field between you, but risk of areas of misunderstanding that cause insecurities and loss of respect

6 in love with a 6 ★★★★★

Two of you together can be wonderful or wishy-washy. Usually it is the former – hence the five-star rating – because **6**s are almost a breed apart in love, showering their mate with affection and kindness, thinking nothing is too much trouble for the one you love. This often results in a truly caring, deep, expansive relationship, where both of you knows exactly what the other needs in terms of support and encouragement. No one knows how fragile a **6**'s ego can occasionally be better than another **6**; and no one sympathizes with the overwork, responsibility and need to be useful that a **6** feels as much as a **6** partner can. Your intuition runs very high together, and you finish each other's sentences.

With another **6** you will feel you are on familiar ground from the first – both sharing the same spark to create a haven of beauty and tranquillity at home, and responding enthusiastically to each other's physical effort in relation to arranging space and company. You will both be good cooks, talented amateur artists or photographers, skilled at crafts and interested in exhibitions, and will probably want to join a local group where you can be part of a wider community of equally creative people. Your music collection will be vast and your budget for a sound system a priority, getting the best you can afford – and knowing it will get plenty of use. Similarly, your budget for the extrasensory things in life – scented candles and quality linens – may also go through the roof. The joy of being with another **6** is that you don't need to explain yourselves to one another.

The wishy-washy scenario comes about if you're too obliging towards one another, neither of you willing to take the lead or be upfront about your individual needs. **6**s can be stubborn and a little sulky if things don't go their way, but sometimes you will feel reluctant to articulate this. One of you must occasionally break the reverie and be decisive, to save the bond from meandering without achievement. An aimless life will fail to bring out the great possibility in the relationship, so – occasionally – one of you will have to get tough!

But the good is truly good: together you lift each other's hopes higher, explore different ends of creativity, and make a wonderfully joyous social network between you to share and enjoy. Two **6**s will be extremely sensuous, and luxuriate together on gentle breaks away in cosseting locations – chic hotels, lovely spas, beautiful countryside, cosy fires, foody experiences. No two people could enjoy these treats more together than the two of you.

If you can negotiate the initial patch of sizing each other up and overcoming the fear of being with someone who sees inside you so deeply, you could then nestle into one another like complementary halves of a walnut, snug in a shell. Give each other space at the beginning, and appreciate those many occasions which will feel like déjà vu, and sooner or later you'll be growing older and plumper together, and sharing a swag of common dreams!

Key themes

A relationship maximizing beauty and creature comforts • Love and gentleness to the fore • Similar tastes and joys, but guard against too much sweetness and not enough determination! • Similar natures could prevent constructive direction or achievement

6 in love with a 7 ★

Your two numbers are going to be at sixes and sevens, of course! (It's interesting to ponder where this expression comes from: it's certainly clear in its meaning of confusion.) **7** has a feeling of intellectual arrogance and a disinterest in banality – which is fair enough, given their delicate sensibility and lack of patience for the public taste. You find this exclusiveness interesting and even attractive, but ultimately restricting. Put simply, **6** gets on with everyone, and is interested in diversity and popular culture, whereas **7** is frustrated by this apparent lack of discrimination.

This isn't a problem initially: **6** sees fascinating **7**, who looks like they need a patient listener and good-hearted person to discover their pain and enigmatic personality. You enjoy food together and, though you have different styles and tastes, you are perfectly capable of extending each other's experience. **6** seems so genuinely peaceable and laissez-faire about the world, attractive and arts-minded, and disinclined to be jealous of others' success or lucky breaks: surely all guaranteed to pique **7**'s interest, for it is so different from the way a **7** responds? And isn't **6** appreciative of **7**'s mind and sharp humour, and **7** admiring of **6**'s aesthetic taste and good looks? Indeed it is so; but after an initial enthralment, the reality of being quite disparate people starts to flavour the relationship, and it all may go sour.

You will look up to **7**, who is intelligent and even aristocratic in their taste and bearing; and **7** admires all that is fluid and generous in you, for they are naturally critical and even self-castigating at times. But this critical factor is part of what disenchants you over time, because you are forgiving and wise in giving everyone you feel drawn to a chance to show themselves in their best light, whereas **7** likes birds of a feather, and is a specialist and a perfectionist: too fussy, perhaps, for easy **6**, not nearly relaxed enough, and very demanding around the home – even for you!

Still waters run deep, and you have an idea that **7** has a captivating personal tale to tell. Quite right; but **7** won't always want to share, or draw a line on the past, or explain a dark mood that momentarily descends. You respect **7**'s wish for peace, but eventually begin to feel walled out. And, as much as you want a beautiful shared space to live in, **7** may be a bit obsessive for your taste. When you want a glass of wine at the end of the day, **7** – depending on mood – will either join in too heartily or be on a detox diet, and force everyone else to accept their opinions on health and lifestyle. You'll put finishing touches to the bathroom with a pretty bunch of scented flowers, but **7** wonders why they're not white, like the liquid soap and hand towels. **7** demands such attention to detail, while you feel life's too short to be so compulsive. And if the **7** happens to be negative or uninspired, or to have had a broken heart once too often, you will feel all alone in this relationship.

Occasionally this pairing works better than its one-star rating – if the **7** has learned from experience to relax a little, and to appreciate what is different in taste, and if the **6** has achieved a lot of self-discipline and maturity about love relationships, and doesn't feel the need to be constantly reassured by **7**'s words of love (which are often not forthcoming). But **7** doesn't notice how controlling it can be, nor how unintentionally brusque. It will depend on how flexible and good-humoured you are as to how seriously any slights are felt. You'll need to be very wise with each other!

Key themes

Both arts lovers who enjoy a cultured life and friends coming by, but **7** needs far more privacy and discerning company • Problems arise if **6** needs emotional reassurances, or if **7** is hyper-critical and controlling

6 in love with an 8 ★★★

With much in common, **6** and **8** are usually close friends. They work well together, **6** softening some of **8**'s over-ambitious tendencies, enticing them to relax a little. But as a love relationship, this is more about physical attraction and magnetism than ongoing peace. **8** definitely appreciates **6**'s air of calm, and their wish to keep things running smoothly; and **6** is impressed with **8**'s sheer ability and capacity to take control in a crisis. But, in personal terms, they're not always headed in the same direction.

8 sees the world profoundly, sometimes complicating the picture too much for your taste; and, although they have something distinct in their personality which suggests quality and professionalism, they can be stubborn and even faithless when the chips are down – especially in human relationships. **8** always wants to seek solutions to every enigma, unable to let things rest, whereas you need to take some things on faith, and tire of the endless delving into thought, politics, personal motivation that fuels **8**'s energies. You will be drawn to **8**'s air of mystery and authority, but they may at times be just too driven and dissatisfied, and find it difficult to relax if work is demanding.

To **8**, you may appear over-indulgent of others' foibles, or too complacent about life. It is your way to let things come to you, which usually works well, too; but **8** must take charge of fate. So, while their intelligence and introspection is a source of pleasure and fascination to you, you will sometimes feel that their priorities are in the wrong place. There is an unintentionally stern aspect to **8** – a bit too grown-up? – whereas **6** has a charming Pollyanna outlook on the world, believing that the present is to enjoy.

But what does work between you works well – and the sexual side of the bond may be very good indeed. It is definitely an aphrodisiac for **6** watching **8** achieve success in difficult situations, and through deep concentration. Loving luxury, you are mesmerized by **8**'s control of the material world, delighted with their usual wisdom in discourse with others. **8** is always the wise and fair-minded judge – an attribute that you look up to. Their generosity fits exactly with your spirit, and you will spoil each other with beautiful quality gifts at opportune moments. And perhaps music will be the greatest bond between you – for **8** alone is almost more musical than **6**. These aspects – drawing each other to higher realms of appreciation – will see the fostering of some very special personal and binding moments.

Don't let **8** quash your enthusiasms for the little things in life: they can be too entrenched in personal difficulties, and forget their sense of humour. And if they have a troubled past be very wary, for **8** has an elephant's memory. Pain may always lurk close to the surface, and only personal achievement may be able to nullify it. **6** simply doesn't want such entanglement.

And why might **8** love you? Who couldn't, if they are protective and you need protection, or if they are too serious and overworked and need hugging, and you are willing to break though their self-imposed asylum? You offer **8** much of what they need, including a cocoon in which to ponder while significant ideas form. **8** sometimes spends part of its life in darkness, from which amazing seeds can germinate. You are able to surround them with the kind of serenity and loving security that helps this process occur. Give them solitude sometimes, and demand a little give and take in return. You may do better than your three stars!

Key themes

6 steadies **8** when there is an emergency or crisis • **8** depends on **6**'s genuine admiring love • **6** expands **8**'s creative imagination, and **8** will probably take the lead • Need to respect each other's vulnerabilities

6 in love with a 9 ★★★★★

This is potentially very powerful. You each have a goodness and a kindness which buoys and intensifies the other's. As a pair, you would be very giving and indulgent to friends in need or people who want your time. **6** helps **9** slow down and become very unselfish, while **9** forces **6** to think a little more deeply about their talents and interests, their future and what will make them happy. **6** is often too easy-going or too much of a dilettante, but **9** has some of the force of personality to make you perfect your gifts a little.

And **9** is drawn to you: your taste, your looks, the way you appear to the world. Enjoying your love of music, theatre and art, **9** may even broaden your scope, for you are very much birds of a feather in this respect. **9** could inspire you to a greater love of literature, a wish to see the whole world rather than stay at home, and make you think about the politics and philosophies of cultures at a distance from your own. And you are able to make **9** a little less restless and sad, lifting their spirits after a stressful day. **9** is so prone to feel others' woes personally, and you understand how to remedy some of this over-identification. Yet, your faith in broad-thinking **9** may force them to pursue their wider ambitions, and together you could make a difference to the world, rather than just beautifying your own.

9 is very introspective at times, and **6** must cope with this. Don't take it personally. And, as people-loving as **6** is, even you may find there are weekends when you don't want a trail of **9**'s mad friends traipsing through your door. You want to make some time for love and tenderness, and **9** needs signals to this effect. You are both dreamy, but **9** can leave the world completely at times, leaving you wondering what you did or said.

9s are often caught up in their subconscious, and forget others' needs of them. Healing, sensitive and gentle, they are nonetheless cerebral sometimes, and will need your greatest patience. If you are a strong home-maker – common to many **6**s – you'll have to accept that a happy home with a **9** requires a back door left unlatched for your lover to wander in when they have finished wandering elsewhere. **9** is not disloyal or a player, but they don't like to feel restricted: **9** is an actor, and their world has many stages. Anyone in love with a **9** has to learn to tolerate – and even enjoy – these various roles.

But let's be honest: this is what drew you to this cabaret person. **9** is so seductive to you, needing love, resisting labels, refusing to be 'normal', yet utterly charming and versatile and high-minded. How can you resist such appeal – almost a youthfulness wrapped up in a wise old mind? And, even when you're obstinate and a little jealous, how can **9** be immune to your beautifying touches and your serene engagement with people and life? You like mutual things, prefer the truth from one another, and can learn from each other. When you are feeling stay-at-home, just let **9** go visit a friend out of town.

If the love between you grows to a lasting tie and you have children, don't forget your **9**'s *personal* needs. **6** often gets tied up with those who need them, children being a prime concern, but **9** needs you too. Keep the relationship precious and give it plenty of air – away from others. Walking and talking together, listening to each other, is one of the things about this match that can work so well. If you lose it, you lose something very unique.

Key themes

A partnership that can really lead to *love* • **9** is intelligent, warm and broad-minded, enlarging **6**'s world • **6** is patient and loving, beautifies **9**'s world, and offers gentle security • Shared interests and compatible styles

6 in love with an 11 ★★★★

We have already looked at your relationship with a pure **2** (*see page 140*), but what does it mean if the **2** happens to also be master number **11** (born on the 11th or 29th of the month)? Is this likely to improve things, or make them worse? The master numbers have a different impact on relationships ...

If you are involved with an **11**, this can truly be an exhilarating partnership, because you offer each other considerable understanding. The side of you that loves to do worthwhile work in the world is adored by humanitarian and noble-minded **11**. No one may lift you to greater heights of what you can do. In fact, **11** will simply refuse to sit and watch you languish, or let other people steal your thunder when you have worked on a project and achieved distinction within it. **11** – so magical and powerful, a leader and eloquent speaker – makes you strive to fulfil your own self. Plain and simple.

If it transpires, however, that you have a master number in common – for example, if your LIFE number (*see page 214*) adds up to either **11** or **22** (before reducing to a **2** of **6**) – it may be the case that you are just too much for each other! **11** needs to be a little in the limelight, and, while they are usually generous and pleased for other people who enjoy success, if they are not expressing their own public-shaking skills at their top level, they may feel sulky and negative. Two master numbers together often make an unstable combination, with one foot on the ground and the other hovering in mid-air. A master number needs someone who is patient and supportive, and who has – above all – faith in them. And this is normally something a **6** can do well.

But one thing you mustn't do is shy away from telling this fascinating and physically magnetic person the truth.

Sometimes an **11** needs somebody to call them out and tell them if they are being unreasonable or lazy, or low-minded or just too self-absorbed. **6** can be so honest and straight-talking, and yet kind at the same time, and this is where your invaluable talent can really come to the fore. Hold the mirror to your **11**, if you will, for you are sure to make a better person of them. Just be aware that, although the world sees them as luminous and infallible, they can also be fragile and sensitive, so it's important to be sincere, but not cruel in any way. Encounters about life, your aims, your hopes and wishes, should bring you both closer together.

If you simply give your **11** a little room to breathe – and maybe give them a brief pep talk every so often, too – miracles may occur. And the love could be superb, fulfilling its four-star potential.

Key themes

A love match with great potential (provided **6** isn't a master number too) • **11** lifts **6** to great heights, and **6** makes **11** a better person • **6**'s gentle honesty is good for **11**

6 in love with a 22 ★★★★

Just as with an **11**, someone born on the 22nd of the month seems to sizzle with cool potential and the promise of escaping a jejune life at any level. **22** also makes things happen, and lures you to love them with their charm and personal presence. You like their 'apartness', their singular way of assessing people and situations, and you forgive them their need to tie things down and make them clearer (a **22** is also a **4**, after all). **22**s will address anyone, from a president to a pig farmer, and ask them – in the same tone of voice – what they mean and what they are doing. **22** is not fazed, and you will enjoy the cast of characters this person brings into your home – and into your thoughts.

Nor will **22** put up with any shilly-shallying from you! You will become much more decisive in company with a

22 lover, whose respect is only given when they find someone with talent, a good heart, a cultivated mind and clarity. If this sounds like a tall order, it is – but a **22** is not for the common palate and, if you are to keep them company for more than a flash affair, you will need to be on your toes! **22** will appreciate all you give – your touches of decorative skill and creative input around the house, your cooking and entertaining skills, your easy way with everyone from the elderly to the tiny tots. You will gain an admirer who notices all of your potential as a human being – not just as a lover.

Now, **22** can be stubborn and – when they get the bug about something – there is no dissuading them. This you will have to live with – and it may make you smile, because you, too, can be like this sometimes. But an enlightened **22** will treasure your patience and goodness, your warmth and calming presence, and you may be able to help them unwind even though few people can. You'll need to accept that with a **22** – and possibly even with an **11** also – your life and time will never be entirely your own. Both of these master numbers concern people who have a duty or mission with groups of people or the wider public, and if you are to fit in you will have to share now and again.

However, the rewards are likely to be worth it, because you will go up a gear in what you set out to achieve in your own life. A **22** will make you try hard, laugh loud, cry at times in fellow-feeling, and maybe sometimes you will need to look them in the eye and bring them back down to earth. But life certainly will be in the fast lane some of the time, and quality one-on-one at others, and this is a balance you can live with.

22's inspirational aura blended with personal practicality may suit you very well indeed. But give it time at the beginning – for a **22** will be like no one else you have dated. Just you wait and see!

Key themes

Both have people skills and must contribute something to the world at the social or cultural level • **22** is very secure for a **6**, and will make **6** feel special, but happiness depends on unselfishness

Work

YOUR **WORK** COMPATIBILITY CHART

	1	2	3	4	5
With a 1	★★★★	★★★★★	★	★★★	★★★
With a 2	★★★★★	★★★	★★★	★★★★	★
With a 3	★	★★★	★★★★	★★	★★★★★
With a 4	★★★	★★★★	★★	★★★★★	★★★
With a 5	★★★	★	★★★★★	★★★	★★
With a 6	★★	★★★★★	★★★★	★★★★	★★★★
With a 7	★★★★★	★★★	★★★	★★★★★	★★
With an 8	★★★★★	★★★★★	★★★★★	★★★	★★★★
With a 9	★★★★	★★★	★★★★★	★★	★★★
With an 11	★★	★★★★	★★★	★★★★★	★★
With a 22	★★★★★	★★	★★★	★★★	★★★★

6	7	8	9	11	22
★★	★★★★★	★★★★★	★★★★	★★	★★★★★
★★★★★	★★★	★★★★★	★★★	★★★★	★★
★★★★	★★★	★★★★★	★★★★★	★★★	★★★
★★★★	★★★★★	★★★	★★	★★★★★	★★★
★★★★	★★	★★★★	★★★	★★	★★★★
★★★	★	★★★★	★★★	★★★★★	★★★★
★	★★★★	★★★	★★	★★★★	★★★★★
★★★★	★★★	★★★	★★★★	★★★★★	★★★★
★★★	★★	★★★★	★★★	★★★★★	★★★★★
★★★★★	★★★★	★★★★★	★★★★★	★★★★	★★★★★
★★★★	★★★★★	★★★★	★★★★★	★★★★★	★★★

5 4 3 2 1 9 8 7 6

6 working with a 1 ★★

1 is a person who wants to make things happen, and this will have one of two possible effects on a **6** in business. Either they may inspire you to believe in your artistic talents and people skills so much that they galvanize you into action, rather than letting you hide behind other more extroverted people; or they may eclipse you into permanent retirement and depression. **6** is sensitive, at home and at work, and needs gentle handling. The result of **1** taking the trouble to do this is that they have a really diligent worker who has much to contribute, because you teach them to feel strongly for others. There will be times, though, when **1** feels you are too soft, or wasting your hours on unworthy causes!

When **1** has a brilliant idea, it is a **6** who can teach that idea – or its uses – to others. As the **6**, you have the diplomacy **1** often lacks, and are willing to take time coaxing people. But your energy levels are quite different. **1** prefers to blazon their way through obstacle courses, while you are opposed to harsh or blustering methods. Sometimes you will have to accept that you see things differently.

Businesses that would feed off the abilities you share are products or services which demand original ideas but offer beauty or comfort for the home, or are related to fashion or food. Here your energies pair up well, and you will discover a mutual respect for each other. The **1** will admire your taste, and often give you precedence in work decisions which need an aesthetic element to succeed.

Key themes

Can please many parties • Draw inspiration from each other • Marry different types of expression

6 working with a 2 ★★★★★

Because of a productive understanding that exists between your numbers, **6** and **2** are very well suited to working in business. **6** has such a delicate understanding of what **2** is doing even without being told, and **2** – always able to compute in an instant where the ground has shifted to – relies on the equally conciliatory **6** to get unwilling customers to agree to just about anything. No other numbers handle individuals better, or have more aesthetic appreciation for making an uplifting environment seem the most desirable place to be. Any work space that houses a **6** and **2** working together will exude a calm beauty where everyone is happy to be.

Add to this the fact that both numbers are creative and like the beautiful things in life – being thus prepared to work steadily for them – and we have a recipe for financial success. Interestingly, there is, perhaps, no natural leader here. You will be as willing to work as **2**'s assistant as they would be to work as yours; this may culminate in a work situation which sees no bosses, but several happy partners!

When you add the two numbers together, we come to **8**: the number of money. Nothing else spells out so well just how much potential these numbers have together, should they go into a business partnership of any kind. Though seemingly quiet and not in the least attention-grabbing, **6** and **2** will seize the day without being noticed. If the direction of the business has anything to do with the beauty industry, music, the arts or teaching/healing, it will be highly successful and happy. A five-star team.

Key themes

Achieve a serene and aesthetically uplifting environment together • Please everyone they deal with

6 working with a 3 ★★★★

A strong understanding and sympathy helps the two of you find a way through all kinds of thorny problems at work. **6** is so visual and caring, and stands back applauding **3**'s talents for making everyone feel better after calamity. And no one gives more time to others than both of you together – with you acting as healer or teacher, and **3** as entertainer and unpaid counsellor. You have a gift for bringing disparate people together and showing others how to get on to greater effect. Work-wise, this is a considerable skill.

3 handles your serious nature without being disturbed by it, because they recognize that it's the product of caring and kindness to others. It's helpful in business, but liable to be oppressing if not alleviated by buoyancy. You look to **3** for guidance when all efforts to avert personality clashes come to nothing. No one can lighten the atmosphere as well as a **3**, and their willingness to turn their hand to any task is inspirational to all. You appreciate their wisdom and sense of proportion.

You should be good at attracting money together, too, and will make the work environment feel beautiful. Both of you place an emphasis on the necessity of getting the aesthetic right – and when it comes to dressing up for the job, you each have contrasting but admirable styles. You will truly respect each other. Don't unwittingly frighten the **3** away from taking big, bold steps. You are more cautious, which sometimes has its place; but it is how you lend each other awareness of what is lacking that makes the work tie between you such a happy and productive one.

Key themes

Complementary relationship shows others how to achieve harmony • Both highly creative • Love of beautiful space

6 working with a 4 ★★★★

Although **6** is the creative artist and **4** the accountant, you two have exactly the right blend of sense and sensuality to make a successful business team. You need just such a person as **4** to stem your panic in a crisis, for you feel pressure personally and can be very difficult to persuade that all will be well. **4** represents the kind of reliable and honest figure that fills you with hope and restores your faith. And **4** is so admiring of your people skills, the fragrant and pretty work space in which you operate, that mutual respect and functionality are bound to result.

A **4** can always calm a **6**'s worries by finding a method that seems obvious once it has been spoken of. You're good at balancing the sensitivities of the rest of the workforce, blending talents and disparate feelings with all the skill of a born counsellor. **4** appreciates this, as it minimizes the disruptions through the office landscape. Metaphorically, **4** produces the solid and well-crafted 'item' for team inspection, and you decorate it beyond the purely functional, until something of real beauty has been born. You make an excellent team, and will be trusted by all.

Money-wise, **6**s are rather lucky in attracting funds and falling on their feet, with well-timed ideas in the marketplace that seem to come without much effort. **4**, though, belies that such effort is invisible – they know how to make the money spin out further, and how to put the real effort in behind the initial 'luck'. So, in financial terms, this is a true marriage of luck and hard grind; and, in personal terms, you will enjoy each other as you go along.

Key themes

Smooth each other's ruffled feathers • Each recognizes what the other needs, and when • Lucky financially

6 working with a 5 ★★★★

You may not be quite sure of the storm that hit you the day **5** arrived in your work arena! Into a sea of tranquillity comes an illuminated pleasure boat, ready to liven things up; and, though this is the antithesis of what you want in your domestic life, in business it is a little bit exciting. **5**'s bombast is good for lethargic **6** – who isn't lazy but inclined to stay out of the line of fire, frequently losing out just to avoid confrontation. They are delighted to do your verbal jousting, and will take many of your good ideas more seriously, and actualize them. And **6** – always patient and kind to all – smoothes over those wrinkles with all the clients and co-workers **5** has no notion they've offended.

You can teach **5**'s brilliant ideas to other, slower, lesser mortals – something **5** is rarely bothered about – and they stir you to become more aggressive about possible goals.

You each boast varied creative abilities – **5**'s more unconventional, **6**'s more traditional; but this means you can combine to appease just about anyone. The real blessing is that you are a pair of opposites who will respect each other. In business, **5** recognizes **6**'s gentle, diplomatic soul, and **6** is determined to find the peace and let **5** have their way.

Businesses that would feed off the abilities you two share are in marketing or public services, real-estate sales and development, publishing or journalism, all of which demand original ideas but offer beauty or comfort. **5** admires your exquisite taste and is grateful for your encouragement concerning their input; give them precedence in work decisions that need an exotic element to succeed.

Key themes

Draw inspiration from one another • Can please many parties • Co-operation essential for your progress

6 working with a 6 ★★★

Working with someone who shares your number, you may be inclined to heighten one another's interests in reform and social improvement: two **6**s accentuate each other's strong feelings of principle. You may gently goad each other to stand up for anyone who is dealt with unjustly, or who is not given a fair chance by society.

Once again, the worst failing will be a mutual meekness and refusal to go after what you need, because neither of you can truly be called an aggressor. The presence of a **5** or a **1** will help here, but do be careful of giving in to the danger of each being so compliant and pleasant about life and work that you may be cheated by competitors or overlooked by clients and peers for important opportunities. Everyone loves you, but not everyone will take you seriously without one of you being the spearhead. Yet you work together on generous acts towards others, without asking for conceited accolades, so you will definitely win people's confidence regarding your honesty and moral integrity.

If you work together in food or fashion, you must surely succeed – though get a **4** to do the accounts! – and, if true to type, you will allow the working day to spill across the early evening into socializing hours. As with love relationships between two **6**s, just be wary of not letting too much sweet acceptance and love of luxury to blunt your purpose. You like money and want pretty things, so the trick will be to harness your considerable gifts, good taste and diplomacy with others' talents, and turn it into profit. It can be done!

Key themes

Many potential lines of enterprise • Will make colleagues feel pampered • Don't let the pursuit of goals dissipate

6 working with a 7 ★

Hmmn … not sure about this one. Your different styles – which can be entertaining in love relationships – could really lead to clashes or suppressed feelings. **6** so rarely lets fly when there is a hurt or slight, preferring to keep everything (and everybody) cheerful; but **7** can't help being biting and critical if anyone is shirking their load. You will laugh sometimes – because **7**'s tongue is razor-sharp and very funny; but this is not how a **6** does business. Where you want to offer someone a chance to get started, **7** doubts they will maximize their chance (possibly only too correctly!), and there will be fallout if **7** is right.

You also undermine **7**'s strategies occasionally, being too causal in your opinion about the way things should be done, or relying too heavily on charm and surface impressions and not seeing deeply into things and people. **6** gives everyone the benefit of the doubt; and **7**, almost no one! Plus **7** is a specialist who likes to work with other perfectionists/specialists, whereas **6** is so capable of dipping into many requirements. **7** won't trust this jack-of-all-trades ability, and may miss out on something very special in your talents by refusing to take you seriously.

7 will appreciate **6**'s artistic touch and understanding of what will be popular in the marketplace, and **6** admires **7**'s focus and determination to know the whole of any subject. Thus, at best, this may become a marriage of opposites, which works well enough, if you give each other space and respect to do things differently. But, methinks, it is walking on eggshells for each of you.

Key themes

6 flatters **7**'s ego but only briefly, finding **7** too sharp • Good intelligence, but clashing styles with potential flare-ups

6 working with an 8 ★★★★

In truth, **8** – the number of business and money matters – works well with most people, so it's no surprise to see a solid tie between two amiable souls. You will have to exercise a little patience now and again, because **8** dances to a different drum to most people and is, well, driven! Sometimes there are other things to do besides work. But you will definitely get ample opportunity to show what you're made of: **8** will really value your more aesthetic and decorative contributions to basic business ventures – whether this means the dressing-up of a product or the flourishes that strengthen bonds with other business people. **8** will trust you to add a certain polish and finesse.

And you enjoy having someone inspiring to be imaginative for. **8** is a number which never doubts any possibility, and you will be empowered by such extraordinary dynamism combined with an inclination to dig to find research and resources. You are dying to show what you can really do, but, lacking a touch of confidence about it, you will bask in **8**'s assurances of interest and commitment. **8** gives you confidence, and you blossom for it.

8 always has a goal – unless they temporarily lose their way through over-extending themselves – and **6** can play a vital calming role in **8**'s business life. Also, **8** already has strong commercial tendencies and an appreciation of the luxury market, and **6** will add a desirable feeling of harmony to the work environment. Overall, this is a powerful tie with a great chance for financial and personal success, allowing you to find your true brilliance in your best field.

Key themes

6 softens **8**'s fervency in a positive way • **8** takes the lead and brings dynamism • **6** packages **8**'s exhilarating ideas

6 working with a 9 ★★★

Probably better suited to a personal relationship than a business tie, the interaction between your two numbers is nevertheless still very positive, and offers a chance for each of you to work at your best individual capacity. **6** won't interfere with **9**'s lofty thinking and forward-planning, nor will **9** forget the niceties that make **6** feel comfortable in a work atmosphere. **6** will always be consulted by **9**, and has much to say. In one sense, **9** has mastery over the words and **6** over the visions; **6** has the ability to see how an end product or service should be presented to the world, but **9** knows whether it has any potential. In tandem, this is good.

A **9** will always make you feel valued as a negotiator and help you to see your own ability at a higher level. **6**s so often let opportunities float away through mild lack of ambition or conflict with personal obligations, but **9** won't stand for this, and will ask you to learn anything that your training may be missing, in order to go up a level.

When it comes to calming down after a stressful situation – perhaps a tricky client or peer group – or a busy day, **6** performs the magic for **9**. A **9** can really feel personally 'wrung out' from difficult conditions, but a **6** has a soothing manner and a good philosophical spin on day-to-day things. In a nutshell, **6** makes daily life at 'the office' more comfortable for **9**, allowing them to think and plan, while **9** ponders the direction in the longer term, and asks for **6**'s gracious companionship in the journey ahead. A very sensible and well-mannered arrangement.

Key themes

Understand what the public wants and how to provide it • Share a love of life outside the office • Good friendship

6 working with an 11 ★★★★★

What is good and progressive in a partnership with a **2** steps up another notch with the master number. Adding **2** and **6** we come to **8**, the number of executive status and money, and adding **11** and **6** we come to the **17** (**1**+**7**) variant of **8**, a number of deeper exploration. As a business tie, therefore, you team up to find solutions to problems through a fusion of bonhomie and good research skills, and an **11** at work will have you dipping deep into your intuitive nature. Together you will gain the reputation of being deep and insightful, inspired and rather luminous. It works.

Ask the **11** to take any ego outbursts (which will come!) out of the work space, and to have any emotional explosions away from you. **11**'s one calamity for a **6** is the potential to disrupt your calm, for **11** *almost* thrives on drama, where you do just the opposite, and need a serene air and harmonious work relationships to function at your best. However, **11** has the advantage of prompting you to think more deeply and carefully, and trusts your inner feelings about others' motives. You act as a shepherd, keeping dangers and distractions away from the **11** when they are deep in thought or feeling introspective about some particular problem. This helps them find the necessary privacy and concentration to sort out even the biggest tangles. **11** needs just such a gentle and uplifting influence as you.

This is a big part of your role, marrying your grace to **11**'s genius, finding ways of negotiating with all kinds of high-profile people. Yours is a powerful business partnership, as long as you demand your quiet space sometimes.

Key themes

Good combined judgement • Mutual respect and trust • **11** needs **6** to be amusing but firm at times

6 working with a 22 ★★★★

The **22** will be pushier than you – and far more self-reliant – so you should synthesize well. In a successful business team it is ideal if one person takes more of the 'softly-softly' approach and the other noses out opportunities and forges ahead after them. Such should be the blend between you two, as a **22** could open doors and then let you do the soft talking once you're in.

22 is glittering and impressive in front of an audience, but perhaps doesn't always listen to the tone of the audience's voice. This is where you step in, fathoming out what is required from a more sensitive or, indeed, prickly client or colleague. Focused on the sunshine outcome, **22** isn't always thinking about a passing rain shower. They never mean to cause offence, but manage it sometimes anyhow!

What is attractive in this work relationship is that you

have the familiarity with individual people's difficulties or needs in all business situations to be able to intimate to each other what is required for success. **22** is watching the bigger picture all the time – to good effect – while you have a sensitivity for the miniature. This is superb team-work, since both of you see opposite sides of what needs doing, or pursuing, or saying. The **22** will be more ambitious and recognize potential pitfalls, but is quite likely to send you in as the deal-maker. And, if anyone thinks you're easy to get around, they haven't seen how stubborn you can be when you feel sure you're right. A **22** will make you sure!

Key themes

22 acts as the 'master' to **6**'s 'apprentice', but misses some of the individual touches **6** adds • A good balance for each other

Friendship

YOUR FRIENDSHIP COMPATIBILITY CHART

	1	2	3	4	5
With a 1	★★★	★★★★★	★★	★★★	★★★
With a 2	★★★★★	★★	★★★	★★★★	★
With a 3	★★	★★★	★★★★	★	★★★★
With a 4	★★★	★★★★	★	★★★★★	★★
With a 5	★★★	★	★★★★	★★	★★★
With a 6	★	★★★★	★★★★★	★★★	★★★★
With a 7	★★★★	★★★★★	★★★★	★★★★★	★
With an 8	★★★★	★★★★	★★★★★	★★	★★★★
With a 9	★★★★	★★★	★★★★	★★★★	★★★★
With an 11	★★★	★★★★★	★★	★★★★★	★★
With a 22	★★★	★★★	★★★★	★★	★★★

6	7	8	9	11	22
★	★★★★	★★★★	★★★★	★★★	★★★
★★★★	★★★★★	★★★★	★★★	★★★★★	★★★
★★★★★	★★★★	★★★★★	★★★★	★★	★★★★
★★★	★★★★★	★★	★★★★	★★★★★	★★
★★★★	★	★★★★	★★★★	★★	★★★
★★★★	★	★★★★	★★★★	★★★	★★★★★
★	★★★★	★★★	★★	★★★★★	★★★★★
★★★★	★★★	★★★★	★★★★	★★★★★	★★★
★★★★	★★	★★★★	★★	★★★★	★★★★
★★★	★★★★★	★★★★★	★★★★	★★★★★	★★★★
★★★★★	★★★★★	★★★	★★★★	★★★★	★★

At ease with almost anyone, you make friends wherever you go, and with people from all walks of life – though some might trample your sensitivity. Let's see which are the best combinations ... and which are the worst:

6 and **1** (★): This is not always so straightforward, as you see **1** with an 'I am' ego and sense of authority, enjoying taking control over others. Plus, they can be a bit peremptory. But when it is really important, you can hold your tongue and listen. And **1** often has entertaining things to tell you.

6 and **2** (★★★★): **2** is as warm with others as you – a little more critical and possibly sulky, if they don't feel appreciated or consulted on important matters. **2** is highly intuitive, and you will value their good insights for your personal life. You enjoy similar things, and are likely to be very close friends.

6 and **3** (★★★★★): You are good company for each other. **3** loves you, and will keep you close and grow with you over time. You enjoy **3**'s humour and aesthetic awareness – which isn't far from your own. A natural friendship, as you listen to each other and both like nights out without romantic complications.

6 and **4** (★★★): A **4** may not be your *best* friend – though you will be quite protective of this sometimes prickly, oft-times traditionally minded soul. Many just find **4** too square and unadventurous, too stoical, but you'll help bring them out of their shell a little.

6 and **5** (★★★★): Don't fall in love, perhaps, but a **5** friend is an energy pill for you. You're really not that similar, and **5** may bruise your sensibility occasionally, but you'll have good fun on a night out with a **5** friend if you let yourself go a little. Pack your dancing shoes.

6 and **6** (★★★★): More fun here – and better, in some ways, than a love affair, which can be a bit like treacle. Basically, you just enjoy the same things: the arts, movies, concerts and dinners out. If one of you has a broken heart, the other will do their damnedest to heal it!

6 and **7** (★★): This is more of a test of your generosity. **7** may be a best friend for many a soul, but for you they are probably on a different planet. **7**s are often caustic and very intolerant, always sure they're right, and you will grow weary listening to their opinion on everything. Find a different friend!

6 and **8** (★★★★): This is a 'pally' relationship; good for both of you. You share each other's taste for expensive luxuries and quality items, enjoy people, and have excellent judgement. **8** may be tougher than you, and also helps you to laugh at relationship blunders. Lifetime friends.

6 and **9** (★★★★): Not quite as good as an **8**, but still worthy of four stars. **9** is sociable and will drag you out when you're feeling low. **9**'s not as intimate with others as you, but you'll have a vast array of extended friendships and enjoy lively discussions once in a while.

6 and **11** (★★★): Fall in love or go into business, but don't be surprised if an **11** friend frustrates you at times. You have plenty to talk about and a very good humour together, but **11** is not always practical and can be a bit selfish – though you may improve that in them?

6 and **22** (★★★★★): You have different ways of saying what you both mean, but this friendship is a strong one. **22** is bolder, while you are more in tune with the miseries of any other people in your party. You would do well travelling together, or even living as flatmates, because you quickly establish a workable order and respect one another.

6 IN OTHER PLACES

So what does it mean when your number turns up on a house? Do you live in a 6 home? And how does the number 6 affect your pet – or even the car that you drive? Numbers exude a subtle influence on everything in our lives; and here are just a few examples of how ...

A 6 address

If the number of your address – or of your apartment – reduces back to a **6**, settle into your love nest. This will feel like the perfect place to be happy in yourself and in your heart – a bright and spacious oasis of calm, even if it's tiny and four floors up on a busy city street. A **6** house or apartment has an aura all of its own.

And could it be better for throwing dinner parties or offering a hostel to friends with something to talk about? Not as frantic as a **5** home or as party-like as a **3**, a **6** domestic environment offers more individuality and cocooning to anyone craving an hour of tender loving care. And, however small it may be, and no matter how grey the day, this space manages to feel secure and friendly and chic – albeit on a budget. A **6** home is ideal for a family or a loving couple, or anyone who wishes to be heading in that direction!

A 6 pet

If you don't know your pet's birthday, use the first letter of their name to calculate their number. If it's an F, O or X, they're a **6**. This is an affectionate being, par excellence. A **6** cat has such a wonderful way of making you feel welcomed when you come in from a long day – and, yes, they are waiting for a dish of food with a pinch of something extravagant added, but this is not to take away from how much they love you and just want a cuddle. And a **6** dog is the one who knows that you need them to be there, to offer just their presence or the option for a pat. Love is what your **6** pet is for.

Soft, and enjoying tactility, your **6** pet likes moderate exercise but also just to snooze in the prettiest corner of the garden or living area, to listen to sweet sounds, to become acquainted with Mozart. Even a **6** horse will jump higher or run faster out of pure love. So, stroke this creature generously, take time to say hello when you come in, and try not to indulge them with too much food – because they're expert at begging for it!

A 6 car

If the numbers of your licence plate reduce to **6**, this stylish car (truly aesthetically beautiful, even if it's just a VW Beetle) doesn't seem suited to taking you anywhere in a tearing hurry. If it's a Ferrari, of course, it will do the miles quickly – but the character of a **6** car asks that you sit back, put on some good music and enjoy the drive.

Whether the sun's shining or not, there is a calming feeling when you get behind the wheel of this loyal little vehicle. Spiritually, the number would be better suited to a Cadillac or a Rolls than a Fiat Cinquecento, but you will find yourself loving this pretty little car and wanting to keep it for years.

YOUR LIFE NUMBER
Your lesson to learn

The time has come to consider the other main number in your numerology chart: your Life Lesson, or LIFE, number. This is sometimes also called the 'Birth Force'. Just as for the DAY number, calculating your LIFE number is easy: simply add together each digit of your full birth date (day, month and year), and keep adding the digits until they reduce to a single number (*see example on page 270*).

And that's it. You have your Life number. So what does it tell us?

What does it mean?

The **LIFE** number takes times to show its mark. You should see its influence over many years, and understand that it is representative of certain strengths and weaknesses that we learn to live with through years of experience. These characteristics need to be analysed over time, and it can take a while for us to come to know ourselves truly from our **LIFE** number. Uncovering these aspects of our character is a process of discovery, and we often don't fully recognize the traits of this number as clearly, or as quickly, as those of the stronger **DAY** number.

Once you have done your sums and discovered this second important number, you'll want to find out what this means. If your **LIFE** and **DAY** numbers are the same, this powerfully reinforces the qualities of your own number, and accentuates both strengths and weaknesses. You won't be fighting corners within your personality by having two numbers to live with that are, perhaps, miles apart in spirit. But then, equally, if your numbers are the same you may lack a broad vision of the world, seeing with very sharp eyes through just a single (though enormous!) window.

On the following pages we will examine what your **DAY** number **6** is like in tandem with each other number, beginning with the powerful doubling of **6 DAY** and **6 LIFE**, and then moving on through all other possible combinations. If you discover you have a **LIFE** number which totals **11** or **22**, before it reduces to a final single digit of **2** or **4**, read the entry for **6** and **2**, or **6** and **4**, but also pay special attention to any extra information given relating to the added significance of the number being a variation of a master number.

SAME **DAY** AND **LIFE** NUMBER

With **6** as the predominant number in your life you are an extremely lovely, gentle and giving person. With a charm and lightness of touch that the Dalai Lama would envy, even if you are a dragon in the business world your steely exterior melts away as you change out of a suit and into a pair of jeans. You are everyone's friend, and, although not always as confident as you would like to be, you take comfort in the knowledge that you are beloved by all. An excellent crowd-pleaser, you don't always realize how multi-talented you truly are.

6 has the people skills demanded of a sophist, with such charm that even Plato could not reprimand you. Your quiet charisma and easy-going demeanour is unquestionably one of your greatest assets, and, in business, if your boss or a colleague wants the signing of a deal to go calmly, they are certain to send you.

Double trouble?

While **6**s appear to be always friendly and relaxed, others are neither fooled by such an exterior, nor would they put such pressure on you as to demand your 'happy face' twenty-four/seven. There is no question that you truly are an easy person to get on with, who would not intentionally pick a fight with anyone. But that does not mean you are without judgement, and while your Goldilocks face makes everyone believe that you're as nice as pie all the day long, your closest friends know you better, and love you for that slightly stubborn or deprecating streak. It is an important feature in your character, and gives you the necessary perspective to see what will be a success in life, and what will fall on its face.

With skills in so many areas, it is sometimes hard for a double **6** to know which direction to pursue as a career – especially if your **LIFE** number is '33' (before you add the digits to reduce it to **6**). But, with excellent instinct, and powers of persuasion that could make a devoted Atkins follower give in to a spaghetti sandwich, you are sure to land on your feet.

6s sometimes feel the pressure to be happy-go-lucky all of the time, and with a double **6** this is, of course, doubly true – but don't let it get to you. Remember that everyone is allowed their grey days, so wear yours with pride. While you are externally a very amenable person, you do have an obstinate, selfish side which can sometimes cause you guilty grief. Don't expect too much from people *all* of the time; they can't always read your mind and buy you the perfect gift, or know that you never eat cake on Wednesdays.

Lessons in love

You are desired or admired by all who meet you, and your effortless charm, unwitting grace and beguiling modesty ensure that your St Valentine's Days are always rose-filled. Make the most of your easy-going nature, and don't over-cosset those around you. People rarely live up to our expectations in love, so don't let yours be *too* high, or you will only be disappointed.

With so much to offer as the amiable achiever, don't let insecurity or an over-zealous desire to do the right thing stop you from playing the game. People love the *you* that they see when you are relaxed and having a good time, surrounded by people who love you. Be sure in this.

6 can sometimes let secret insecurity keep them from doing things that they would really like to do. If you want to dance on the tables, just go for it – you've probably got the legs, anyway! And if you want to tell your boss they're wrong, do so! It will sound better coming from you than from anyone else.

Friends reunited

With talent, charm and affability on your side, you have so many friends that people will be flying in from all around the world for your sixtieth birthday – and you can be sure they will have checked what colour the wrapping paper is meant to be, so as not to disturb your colour scheme. With your toes in so many ponds there are a multitude of things that you could excel at, and your personable nature guarantees that you will make all the right connections to do well in whichever field you choose.

Above all, be confident, have fun, and moderate your expectations of others just a little, and then you are sure to enjoy yourself. Go out there and live life to the full – the way that only a **6** can.

DIFFERENT **DAY** AND **LIFE** NUMBERS

Most of us will find that we have two different birthday numbers, and this can be an advantage. One number may soften the single track of the other, and mean we can see other people's viewpoints more easily. At other times, though, the numbers may be in real conflict – and this leads to vacillation in our reactions to everyday situations, or confusion about why we want to run one way and then another.

In the following pages you will discover how your own two numbers are likely to work together, and what you can do to maximize the potential of both when they are paired up.

6 Day with 1 Life

These numbers might discomfit each other, coming together in two different people meeting at a party, but working as the two principal numbers within a single individual they seem to donate richly diverse talents from opposite sides of the numerological 'gene pool', and make a greater whole for it. As one number is a generous giver and the other an unabashed taker, if these are your two numbers you have the best of both worlds. You will know when to look and when to leap; you have creative patience and the self-discipline to be a good learner and an even better teacher, but you also have the confidence to act on your feelings, and you know how to tackle impossible situations. If **6**'s problem is often to give too much ground to others, or be self-sacrificing to a personally damaging degree, the self-worth that comes with **1** saves you.

Equally, the **6**'s inherent sensitivity prevents the abrasive hurtfulness that **1**s usually cause without intending to.

Both numbers are creative, but the **6** is truly artistic, so the pairing of capabilities is very likely to express itself in the arts. Also, study will be a naturally desired pastime, with many people marvelling throughout your lifetime at how much you know in a variety of disciplines. **6** is always gently curious, and **1** has the decisiveness to investigate any situation if it doesn't know the answer. This promotes a good balance for your intellectual focus.

In romantic matters, the **6** softens **1**'s instinct to be alone, and of being unsure how to ask for – or give – love. **6** is the very number of love, and having both numbers makes emotional feelings less of a problem. That said, however, **6** must be loved at all costs, and **1** has impossible standards for a partner to live up to, so you will probably be very choosy before you eventually settle down.

Shared traits between the numbers include artistic

and aesthetic appreciation, and a sense of idealism about what can be done in the world ... while on the contradictory side, **6** loves domesticity and has stubborn, slightly conventional opinions, whereas **1** is a freedom-lover and wants to move forwards. Resolving these differences is going to be the interesting bit, and it won't always come smoothly; but it does mean that you will often surprise even yourself in your reactions to emotions, dramas and events. Maturity may make it easier for you to know which way you'll jump in a crisis!

6 Day with 2 Life

These numbers are made for each other, and will entice the best qualities in each to greater performance, working in tandem for you. **6** is so creative and peace-loving, and has, like **2**, such good taste and an artistic eye, that it is hard to imagine you would be drawn to do anything else but work in an artistic career. Music, acting, painting are talents that come with each number, so when these numbers come together they will have a very strong impact, and highlight such talents artistically in so many different areas. Both **6** and **2** are numbers that make good teachers, health workers, community professionals, and these fields of opportunity may also attract you vocationally.

What a loving home you will create, and what a concentration on the *needs* of those you love. Surely, with this pair of numbers, you will spoil your children, support their dreams, stand up for them when they suffer injustice? And challenging your mind will also seem crucial, because both **6** and **2** like to get their teeth into research and reading. **6** and **2** together make a person who is both dreamy and a dream-maker; you are attentive to what is in the minds, hopes and hearts of the people around you, and you'll spend time and energy constantly trying to make wishes really come true for someone you love ... for which reason, you may sometimes be a little extravagant financially, or never know when enough is actually enough!

These two numbers are generally so agreeable that it is hard to imagine how they could have anything but a serene and beautiful impact on a person's character, as they come together to influence you. Most at fault, then, might be that **6** and **2** are a little too passive, or that these numbers fail to prop each other up with any aggression – which can be needed sometimes. Or, it may be that you are too idealistic and gullible, at times. But this seems a small price to pay for the gifts of charm, taste, creativity and understanding that come with your numbers, so try to surround yourself with those who won't take too much advantage, but will simply be honoured to share your calm and gracious space, and just to live near you.

Being a number-combination that will prioritize entertaining and having company, or being a really good cook rather than just a competent one, make sure you don't overdo your lifestyle with too much good food or soft living. It is, perhaps, the worst danger that comes from both numbers together – especially if the **2** is an **11**.

6 Day with 3 Life

The most domestic variation for any number **3**, a **6 DAY** number concentrates your **3 LIFE** number energies on creating a perfect home that is beautiful, functional, and a haven for everyone to visit. You will adore your children, and be permanently inspired with ways to create a feast for their senses – **6** prioritizing family, as it does, and **3** the best number at romping on the floor with toddlers to teens.

Your ability in the pure arts is pronounced, especially with a gift for design and fashion, but also with a strong taste for drama and music. You may prefer to work in an artistic field from home, if possible, but **3** saves **6** from its inclination to close off from the world at times. Though **6** is serene, **3** is vibrant, and a blending of these characteristics will set the style for your life pattern. Sometimes outgoing, sometimes introverted, you will surprise yourself with your varying taste for whether to stay in or hit the town.

One of **6**'s failings is to be obstinate or overly traditional, but here **3** comes to the rescue, making you more inclined to react to testing circumstances with some flexibility, and to try new things rather than retreat to the familiar. Equally, **6** calms **3**, and allows you to feel that time spent on recreation and relaxation is justified, especially if this means you can indulge your family in luxuriant pursuits shared with them alone. You will undoubtedly be a good cook, as happy catering a children's birthday party or a picnic in the woods as tea with the vicar or a visit from the in-laws. You can gauge the requirements of any situation to the letter, and have an uncanny knack of choosing exactly what is right for any occasion. And you are renowned for your skill at choosing a perfect gift for a quirky individual, or saying the right thing to a friend in a crisis. Sensitivity combined with originality are the cornerstones of your personality.

At some point in your life you may go through a crisis of identity, where you must decide how it is that you would like the world to see you. It will affect everything: your choice of career and selection of partner. Your sense of yourself is very important, and you don't like to be labelled by others. **6** is very sensitive to making a good impression and cares what the world thinks, while **3** needs to be seen as charming and a good person. If you feel you are being underestimated by anyone around you, it will create a deep wound. For this reason, take time and care about your educational choices and where you want to be in the world. You need to respect yourself, and, with this achieved, you will always draw gracious respect in turn from everyone around you.

6 Day with 4 Life

6's charm, exercised daily, will have a wonderfully uplifting effect on the dryer character of the over-branching **4**. Perhaps **4**'s most disarming failing is an ability to articulate the truth to friends without tact at times – bluntness being a **4** trademark, but not something that is always welcome at any given time. **6** ameliorates this tendency, allowing **4** to be honest and stay true to their moral compulsion for truth, yet softening this with a verbal gentleness and a feeling for the way in which necessary truths might be couched.

4 deepens **6**'s role as counsellor and good friend, helping especially in relationships, where **4**'s need for openness is sometimes at odds with the other person's ability to express what *they* are feeling. **6** lends **4** more politesse, and also makes **4**'s practical and questioning nature seem far less brittle.

Actually, **6** is an ideal **DAY** number partner for **4** life, helping to catalyse **4**'s considerable creative ability with more of a flourish. **6** has such a genuine eye for artistic treasures and aestheticism, and a **4** with a **6** as the partner birthday number will have more taste and take more time to create a visual balance alongside the utility of an object or space. **6** broadens **4**'s horizons, and **4** lends the sometimes fragile temperament of a **6** more solidity. Here is a person who is likely to be a talented cook, and have a practical but also *beautiful* home and garden.

The danger quantity, with these two numbers influencing you, is that your sense of duty and familial – or even social – responsibility may be taken to extremes. You could wear yourself out in the care of others. This is not practical, but some of **4**'s over-practicality does soften under the gentler heart of **6**, which is often selfless (but not always for your own good). Try to find a balance between duty and kindness on the one hand, and self-worth and personal need on the other. You could achieve much that is real and solid, but which speaks to the practical world with beauty and grace. The **4** makes you much more grounded, and yours are gifts worth expressing.

6 Day with 5 Life

It would be hard to find two more different numbers! While **5** wants a constant party with a live jazz band and an open bar, **6** wants a night at the opera. **6** requires peace and tranquillity, while **5** insists that the party never stops. The conflict of these two numbers means that you have two very different sides to your personality. On the one hand, your **LIFE** number – which you will grow into more and more – makes you a fantastically enthusiastic party-lover who is friends with everyone, completely laid-back and loving of life. But on the other hand, that everyday **6** side of your personality means that you often require solitude, and like to be given the time to focus your attention completely on one activity without interruption.

This combination makes for an explosive person whom everybody loves and admires. Behind **5**'s incredible drive and artistic flavour, **6** allows you a little more balance and *sense* in every action. **6** anchors the frenetic **5**, ensuring that jobs get finished and projects are achievable. **6** gives you the head for business, but **5** knows how to make things happen. Your party-planning business is the best around, with **5**'s unquestionable flair for colour, life and partying combined with **6**'s more cautious business head. However, **6** can be a particularly stubborn number at times, and, while **5** makes the somewhat unbending **6** a little less uptight, **5** can be just as demanding and unrelenting when pushed. This means that it is not uncommon for the usually laid-back **6** to be doubly wilful and unmoving.

5 gives you flair in everything, but **6** sobers **5**'s sometimes wacky fashion sense and, instead of wearing outfits for effect, ensures that you are always beautifully turned out. Although **6** is often the rambunctious **5**'s saving grace, you tend to be indecisive, torn between the outrageous decision and the pragmatic one. **6** governs **5** in a crisis, giving you a level head while other **5**s may fall; but then, **5** gives **6** courage. And **5**'s affability combined with **6**'s nurturing skills makes you a very loyal and helpful person to know. Yet, **5**'s inability to try things that bore them sometimes comes into conflict with **6**'s grafting attitude.

Extremely useful and willing at DIY, great pleasure is taken in working on something with your hands. Being left alone to re-shelf a pantry would be the ideal weekend activity for a **6/5**, who enjoys the practicality of the work as well as the solitude of working alone. The conflicting numbers will mean you love the quietude of the country but feel the beat of the urban grind in your blood, and **5**'s energy puts **6**'s mind for business to excellent use.

6 Day with 7 Life

There's serious taste and style here! This is an explosive combination of numbers, with **7**'s quick wit and sharp tongue giving **6**'s enviable people skills the forum to be displayed at their best. You are a raconteur par excellence, and everyone wants to be near you. There is a charm and sparkle about **7** which your **6** makes accessible – softening the bite! – and, with invitations to your best friend's birthday and the Black and White Ball alike, you are sure to delight all with your humour and charisma. There is a magic about **7** that makes it an alluring and yet frightening number to be around. It is not uncommon for people to take offence at **7**'s wittily cutting remarks, but here **6** saves the day, with its masterful people skills and basic kindness, ensuring that everyone can laugh at themselves.

7 adds determination to **6**'s natural aptitude for so

many things, and this combination of numbers is not uncommon in managing directors, politicians and chair-people. Better at making something out of other people's creative works rather than your own, **7** adds a steely business sense to **6**'s eye for beauty. It really is a powerful pairing of numbers, with **6**'s persuasive talents (watch them sell a signed Mick Jagger picture to a Beatles fan using gentle charm!) and **7**'s killer instinct when it comes to business. You are destined to be modelling the latest trends in the newest sports car, the next time you pull up at the tennis club. **6**s are by no means lacking in ambition, but **7** provides the necessary nous to drive home the advantage where **6** might otherwise shy away.

Though each can be surprisingly retiring at times, **7** added to **6** bestows the confidence to carry off those skyscraper heels without flinching, and to approach the sexy Martini-quaffer in the bar with effortless grace. But **6** also mellows the often cheeky **7**'s need for a challenge –

perhaps making you content just to have a quiet drink with rallying friends, instead of running off to the club to publicly admonish a faithless lover or a disappointing business associate. **7** gives **6** that lift which makes you a bee with a killer sting. **6** may hold their tongue in public, but **7** certainly never will!

There is no question that a **6/7** combination is not to be trifled with. Your stellar instincts make you queen of the office or king of the cartel, while your smooth moves and easy manner ensure you are surrounded by people. Take advantage of your natural attributes and work your **7**'s sharpness. You have **6**'s sweetness to convince the traffic warden you really didn't realize loading bays were for industrial deliveries, and not just for quick purchases at Manolo Blahnik.

6 Day with 8 Life

This is an extremely lucky combination of numbers, as **8** can sometimes be a bit of a dragon to contend with, but **6** gives you the gentle personableness necessary to put your fire-breathing techniques to best use. While **6** often prefers to contribute to other people's creative skills, **8**s have more meteoric aspirations of their own, not content to watch others do a job they know they could do better. They will always jump head first into a project that they are convinced will be a success – and with a **DAY 6/LIFE 8** pairing, you are usually right. **6**'s ineffable charm and peace-making skill gives **8**'s power of eloquence and entrepreneurial talent the scope to soar – and the sky doesn't even begin to be your limit. You could take control of your world like a baby tycoon dominating a Monopoly board – cool and unnoticed until you've cleaned up!

6's skills in so many areas can sometimes be a burden, but **8** channels the creativity into exciting and enticing new projects. **6** will have met and charmed the next big thing in the art world in a small café in Soho, but **8** makes certain they are signed to your publishing company before the lattes have even arrived. **8**s are charming and versatile all on their own, but that is intensified in this pairing. **6**'s easy-going attitude, which puts everyone at ease, is combined with **8**'s electric appeal and occasional necessary ruthlessness to make a captivating person everyone is in awe of.

Despite **8**'s unquestionable charm and visible 'outsider' appeal, they can often be very deep and private people, and are certainly stubborn and unrelenting characters once 'in the groove'. In a **6/8** pairing, **6**'s sometimes selfish stubbornness can be magnified to make you a little unbending at times, and you need to remember that not everyone sees things as plainly as you do. **6** will never complain openly about the silly or cheap choice of gift someone has given them, or the inadequacy of the thanks received for a favour rendered, but **8** will make such complaints clearly heard through other discreet but punitive means. (The lesson here, if you know a **6/8**, is to be sure to pick a small tasteful present of good quality for their birthday!)

What is excellent, though, is that **6** reins in **8**'s impatient nature to make sure that, even though **8** has no time for fools, the necessary care is taken to gather information from odd sources. **6** and **8** are both very personable, and this combination really is beloved by those who know you. You are friendly and sympathetic, and always have reservations at the best restaurants. But even the affable **6** has moments when the fire-breathing **8** in you rears its head! Enjoy it: how often do we get to say exactly what we want?

6 Day with 9 Life

Being the last number of the cycle, any number-pairing with **9** usually means that you are good at seeing things through to the end, and this is very important for multi-talented **6**, who can so easily get lost in the vast number of things that they are good at. With a **6 DAY** number, **9**'s sometimes depressive or reclusive tendencies are swept away and replaced by **6**'s trademark geniality. But then, **9** adds practicality to **6**'s skill, and gives a different depth to the easy-going **6**.

With **9** on your side you are bound to succeed at anything you turn your hand to. **6**s have the friends, the social invitations and all the good humour to ensure you get meetings with the right people to help you to your purpose. **LIFE** number **9** adds the necessary vision that makes your **6** dreams a reality, and allows you to envisage an end use for your diverse range of talents. Given half a chance, **9** can demonstrate extraordinary people skills itself, being a good public speaker and big-brother figure to everyone; and **6** is just the gentle but upbeat other half it needs. **9**'s sometimes critical, and silently severe, opinions are partially calmed by **6**'s forgiving nature, making you a really lovely, charitable person to have on side.

Relationships are not always the easiest thing for a **6/9**, as both numbers bring numerous friends and admirers, but possibly no one you would trust your heart to. And **6**'s occasionally shy behaviour is allowed to run riot a little by **9** – not known for its vivacity. Whereas **6** can be so stubborn, headstrong and demanding when provoked, **9** is more flexible, and quietens these hidden demons, making you an easy-going friend. But don't let **9**'s mildness stop you from expressing your emotions now and again, and don't become trapped in a dutiful/reliable role with someone, when you would naturally prefer to give rein to a sexier, more sultry persona with a racy heart!

9 is a very wise number, and this diminishes the amount of secret complaining and perceived frustration that the number **6** is entitled to – offering new perspective on everything ... although, with **6** as your **DAY** number there is no doubt that your generous nature would usually win out eventually anyway. **9** pulls the sometimes stay-at-home **6** out into the world more, and, with talents up to your armpits, you are certain to be a success at what you do. But be sure to make the most of your many assets instead of waiting for good things to come to you!

THE FUTURE

Take a look what's in store...

And now we come to the calculation of your future. Each year, on your birthday, you move into a new sphere of number-influence which governs that year. The numbers progress in cycles of nine years; after nine years, the cycle starts over again, and a whole new period of your life begins afresh. The cycle can be applied to every number, so you can discover what the main issues will be for partners, friends and family, as well as for yourself, in any given year (*see calculation instructions, opposite*). Emphasis is placed on what will happen to you when you are in your own year number – that is, in any '6' year cycle.

Working out your cycle

To find out what year you're currently in, use the same formula employed for calculating the **LIFE** number, but substitute the current year for the year in which you were born. Every year, the cycle then moves on by one more number until, after a **9** year, returning to **1**, to begin the cycle again.

Calculation example 1

BIRTHDAY: 24 May 1980

TO CALCULATE THE CURRENT YEAR NUMBER: 2+4+5+ [2+0+0+7 (CURRENT YEAR)] = 20, and 2+0 = **2**

This means that on 24 May 2007 you would move into a ***2*** *year. On 24 May the following year, this would then move into a* ***3*** *year (2+4+5+2+0+0+8 = 21, and 2+1 =* ***3****), and the year after that, a* ***4*** *year, and so on.*

Calculation example 2

BIRTHDAY: 15 October 1961

TO CALCULATE THE CURRENT YEAR NUMBER: 1+5+1+0+[2+0+0+7] (CURRENT YEAR) =16, and 1+6 = **7**

This means that on 15 October 2007 you would move into a **7** *year. On 15 October the following year, this would then move into an* **8** *year (1+5+1+0+2+0+0+8 = 17, and 1+7 =* **8***), and the year after that, a* **9** *year, and so on.*

Many numerologists feel that the impact of a year number can be felt from the first day of that year – in other words, from 1st January. However, the usual school of thought is that the new number cycle is initiated *on your birthday itself*, and my experience tends to corroborate this. So, if your birthday is fairly late in the year – November or December, say – this means that you will have gone through most of the calendrical year before *your* new number-year cycle for that year begins.

Look back over some recent years, and see if – in the descriptions on the following pages – you can pinpoint the moment when your yearly number-cycle for any given year became apparent. You'll be amazed at just how accurate this system seems to be.

A 1 year

This is the perfect time to set up new and quite specific long-term goals, and consider just where you want to be a few years from now. You will have new people around you from this point on, and fresh ideas about them and the interests they awaken in you. This is a completely new chapter in your life, and you should set goals for a better and more fulfilling future.

Career-wise, a **1** year often occurs at a time of new employment, or of a complete change in direction in your working life. You are probably wanting to develop new skills or make use of untested talents. You have to believe in yourself now. This is the time when it's a little easier to step back and see how to get started along a particular path. Goals, you will understand, are perfectly attainable, even if a year ago they seemed unrealistic. In a **1** year you have tremendous focus and independence, and excellent determination.

The secret to your success now is in your ability to concentrate; but, emotionally, things can be quite testing. No matter how strong a love bond may be in your life, a **1** year demands that you do much for yourself. You could feel isolated or unsupported, even if someone dear is close by. This is a test of your own courage and inner strength. Only your strongest desires will gain results ... but then, your desires should be fierce during this cycle. Try not to act impulsively, as the push to do so will be powerful, but also, don't be afraid to be independent and go your own way. Strong urges are driving you – forward, for the most part – and a **1** year lends you exceptional clarity and energy.

A 2 year

A year which demands co-operation and partnerships at every level, **2** is a gentle year cycle, when you can consolidate what you started in the previous twelve months. You will need to be diplomatic and sensitive towards other people's feelings, but your intuition is very strong now, and you are able to share the load and the initiative more than you were allowed last year. For this reason, don't try to push things too far or too fast. After the previous whirlwind year, this is a moment to take your time and get things right.

Relationships come more into focus during a **2** year. This is especially pleasing if someone new entered your life in the last year or so, for the vibration of **2** helps a bond to strengthen, and a feeling of mutuality improves now. In some ways you may feel the desire or the need to

be secretive, but this is because there are unknown elements at work all on fronts. It will affect you at work and at play, and in a close tie you will discover new tenderness that will probably separate you from other friends. If there is no one special currently in your life, this may be the year to find someone: a **2** year brings a relationship much stronger than a fling!

Your negotiation skills and ability to guess what another person is feeling may work very well for you this year; and, if the number **2** derives from master number **11** (which it almost surely will), there is a chance for serious partnerships and master opportunities. You will need to look at contracts carefully, and spend time on legalities. But this is often the most exciting and unusual year out of the nine. Mysteries come to light, and your ideas flow well. Just be prepared to consider another person in every equation.

A 3 year

Time for you! This twelve-month period is concerned with developing your abilities and testing your flexibility. Your imagination is especially strong, and you may have particular opportunities to improve your wealth and make lasting friendships. You will also need to be focused, because the energy of a **3** year is fast and furious, and may make you feel dissolute. Usually, though, this is a happy year spent with some travel prospects and many creative inspirations. Difficulties which intruded in the previous two years are often resolved in this year cycle.

Business and your social life often run together in a **3** year, and work will be a lot of fun. It is worth taking time over your appearance and indulging yourself more than usual, for the sociability of this number brings you many invitations and a chance to create a new look, or to explore other aspects of your personality. You have extra charm this year, so try to use it where it is needed.

Many people find that the number **3** expresses itself in a year cycle as a third person to consider: frequently, this is the birth of a child or an addition to the family, but it might be that another party pressures you in your personal relationship. Don't talk too much about this, or show nervousness. Under a **3** vibration, it is easy to become exhausted – even through over-excitement – so be alert to the impulse towards extravagance and fragmentation. Try to enjoy the way in which you are being drawn out of yourself this year, and allow yourself time to study, write, paint. Anything you really want you can achieve now – even strange wishes and desires can be pulled towards you. Make sure you think a little about what you are asking for!

A 4 year

A much-needed year of good-housekeeping – on the personal level, as well as literally. This year will demand practicality from you. Often a **4** brings a focus on money or accounts, on repairs around the home, or on putting your life into better order. It may not be what you want, yet it will force itself upon you. It is sometimes a year spent with a pen in hand – writing lists or cheques, doing sums and keeping diaries. It is also a year when you will need to do some research, to find out about what you don't know.

You have so much work to do in a **4**, or **22**, year – more than for a long time. Your personal pleasure takes second place to requirement, and it may seem difficult to stick to the task sometimes. Money demands that you do so, for extra expenditure is not advised in this twelve-month period. Yet if this sounds stressful, it also gives you a feeling of satisfaction that you will achieve so much this year – a job of hard work and dedication really well done. It may be that this year gives you a very good foundation for the future and sets up lasting improvements.

You will never survive a **4** – or, especially, a **22** – year if you are not organized and implement a system of work and life. Be honest in what you do with others, but also in what you do for yourself. You cannot deceive yourself, and must check details carefully. You may have a feeling of burden at times, but there is a chance to feel you have done something extraordinary, too. Translate your clever ideas into practical results. The most significant thing for you to do is to concentrate on proper personal management. The weight of the world is on your shoulders, but you can bear it if the preparations you make are good. There is no escape from demands on your time and intelligence, but nothing can be hurried, so face the job ahead and you will soon find you have climbed a hill to new vistas.

A 5 year

After careful management of your time last year, and a feeling of being tied to the wheel, this will seem like bursting from the inside of a darkened room into bright light. Now you have a change from routine to madness, and you may feel a personal freedom that was denied you last year. Nevertheless, nothing is completely settled in a **5** year, and this uncertainty may take its toll. Try to look at this cycle as a chance to find success in newer areas, and a way to advance from necessary stagnation into running waters of energy and vitality. You will update your sense of yourself during this period, and make progress towards the life you want, following the previous year's required self-discipline.

You are admitting to the need for new pastures, so your ideas of what your life might include, or who may have a role in it, may alter now. No one likes to be held back in a **5** year, but it is still important not to be too hasty in your actions. Use your energies, by all means, but govern them with your head. This is the time for innovation, and new takes on old goals, but if you quarrel with those dear to you, or with whom you work, it may be difficult to repair later. If change is still inevitable, be as kind and constructive as possible, and make sure you aren't leaping from one difficult situation straight into another. You need to discover your versatility and personal resourcefulness to get the best out of this cycle. And, for some of the twelve months, travel or lots of movement seems inescapable.

This year is potentially some kind of turning point for you. Learning how to adapt to sudden circumstances is vital, because any plans or directives set in stone will cause you pain, and possibly come unstuck. Be prepared for changes and, if this brings a nervousness with it, try to meet the adventure head-on. If you talk yourself up and take on a front-running position, you can work wonders in a **5** year.

A 6 year

In this, your own year, love is in the air. Other things seize your time too – your home needs attention, and duties demand your energy – but, principally, this year is about emotions and relationships. Sometimes love and happiness are a reward for surviving so much in the past two years, and for unselfish service and support for others. The emphasis is on finding harmony with others, and this may come in various ways. This year, you may have the impetus and opportunity to erase problems that have previously beset you. You understand, and feel acutely sensitive towards, others, and are more radiant than you have been for some time. If you can be kind and positive in emotional dealings, you will benefit in many ways, including materially.

There are hurdles in a **6** year in connection with obligations you feel towards others. At times you are stretched, because there are personal desires and ties you want to nurture which are countermanded by the duties you are subjected to. You may resent this, yet, if you can remain cheerful, you will be rewarded in ways not immediately apparent. Love is trying to sweep you off your feet, but your health may suffer because you are trying to fit in so much, and the intensity of your feelings is strong.

While it's good to be helpful in a **6** year, don't allow yourself to be taken advantage of, or let people drain you completely. Set up a system that lets you delegate some responsibility. Your home may bloom while you're in such a happy mood, and you should feel creative and mellow. The events of a **6** year are not as fast and furious as the previous year, but things move steadily towards a happier state of being. Let the time go as it will, because this is not a year to fight against what comes to you; get into the right philosophical gear and open yourself to pleasant surprises that come from being useful, and being warm with others.

A 7 year

This year is a time for manifesting your goals by visualizing them. See yourself triumphing and continuing toward your vision. Never lose sight of what you want, or confusion will reign. You'll be tempted this way and that, annoyed by gossip, and attacked by those who love you but don't understand what you are trying to do. Don't be swayed by them, or you will lose your opportunities and precious time.

Keep your head, as everything depends on your state of mind. Refuse to react to distractions, and avoid hasty actions or sudden decisions. A calm approach is the best remedy to the chaos surrounding you. You may have to move house without warning, but take it in your stride and make a calm, clear choice on where to go. If you are travelling somewhere exotic, be prepared with vitamins and medicines to avoid viruses of any kind.

Legal matters may arise during this year, relating to business, investments or house options. Consult an expert to avoid pitfalls, and, when you feel happy, proceed with confidence. If you have taken all the facts and details into account, you'll now be within sight of your goal. But watch your health, as the number **7** is connected with this subject for both good and ill. You might get fit and lose some weight or, conversely, suffer with some little grievance. This is a time for mental, spiritual and physical detoxing. Also, rest: take a vacation to the country, to a quiet location where you can think in peace. Let no one confuse you. You may have to wait, but you will know how to come out on top if you listen to your intuition.

This is an excellent year for study, research, writing and reading, and clearing out all the unnecessary people or ideas from your past.

An 8 year

This cycle brings the possible finding of a soulmate. If you're single, you could not have a better chance of meeting that special someone than now. **8** years also relate to money, so you may be caught up with an impossible workload and regard the arrival of such a potentially strong love as poor timing – and perhaps this is why it comes to you, because your attention being taken up elsewhere may be the best reason for someone's admiration. The love vibration you experience under karmic year number **8** may point to a future relationship prospect which has a lasting importance.

For those in settled relationships, pregnancy sometimes comes with this number, and it brings a very special link between the child and their parents. Or, you may experience a deep urge to study a subject that comes easily to you, though you have never learned about it before – a language, perhaps, or an artistic skill you were attracted to but never developed, but which you now pick up well. Even a professional subject that you seem to grasp quickly will seem more important to perfect than ever before. Partly, this is because **8** year cycles concern making more money, and dealing with the deeply felt past. There are huge opportunities for you in an **8** year, and you will want to be prepared to maximize them. However, you'll need to use good judgement and be efficient with your time management.

Many people feel pushed to the limit in an **8** year, because there is just so much going on. Consider, though, that the vibration of the number wants to find positive expression, so the more efficiency and determination you can bring to it, the better the chance of finishing on a high note. Don't over-commit your time or money, and be ready to acquiesce to others' ways of doing things. You need to be confident, but ready to adjust too. **8** is made up of two circles, asking 'infinity' of you. But this year, you can do it!

A 9 year

Your personal affairs all come to a head in a **9** year, and whatever has been insufficient, or unsatisfying, will rise to the surface and demand change now. It could be the fulfilment of many dreams, for this is the culmination of nine years' experience. Whatever is jettisoned was probably no longer of use – though this might seem dispassionate. Many friendships will drift away, but you have probably outgrown them. The strongest demand of you is a readiness to discard what will not be part of your serious future – and this can mean a temporary feeling of insecurity.

You will certainly travel in a **9** year. Even if a trip is short, or of no great distance, it will settle something in your mind. The more compassionate, tolerant and forgiving you are, the more warmth and generosity will come to you. This is not the right moment to start something completely new, but if events arise as a natural conclusion to what has gone before, this is a good thing. Your mind needs to engage with bigger issues, for selfishness or petty ideas will cause you unhappiness under this number. People will thwart you in your career and personal matters – and these obstacles seem to come out of the blue, and are beyond your control. However, if you think on philosophical issues and remain open to big ideas, everything will turn out well.

A **9** year can be populated with many friends and activities, yet can feel lonely too; this is a cycle for completion of tasks and the ending of what is not enduring. But this is the right time to see the fruits of your previous work. Be wise about where your destiny seems to want to take you. Your artistic and imaginative facilities are inspired now, and you'll begin to see new directions that you know you must investigate in the years ahead. You know what is missing in your life, or where you've failed yourself, and can now prepare for the new adventure that's about to dawn.

How to find your DAY NUMBER

Add the digits for the day of birth, and keep adding them until they reduce to one number:

EXAMPLES

24 May 1980	2+4 = **6**
15 October 1961	1+5 = **6**

How to find your LIFE NUMBER

Add the digits for the day, month and year of birth, and keep adding them until they reduce to one number:

EXAMPLES

24 May 1980	2+4+5+1+9+8+0 = 29 2+9 = 11 (a 'master' number), and 1+1 = **2**
15 October 1961	1+5+1+0+1+9+6+1 = 24, and 2+4 = **6**

Further reading

The Complete Book of Numerology, David A. Phillips, Hay House, 2006

The Day You Were Born: A Journey to Wholeness Through Astrology and Numerology, Linda Joyce, Citadel Press, 2003

Many Things on Numerology, Juno Jordan, De Vorss Books, 1981

Numerology, Hans Decoz and Tom Monte, Perigee Books, 2001

Numerology: The Romance in Your Name, Juno Jordan, De Vorss Books, 1977

Sacred Number, Miranda Lundy, Wooden Books, 2006

The Secret Science of Numerology: The Hidden Meaning of Numbers and Letters, Shirley Blackwell Lawrence, New Page Books, 2001

About the author

Titania Hardie is Britain's favourite 'Good Witch' and a best-selling author. Born in Sydney, Australia, Titania has a degree in English and Psychology, and also trained in parapsychology and horary astrology. With a high media profile, she regularly appears on television in the UK, US, Canada, Australia and South Africa, as well as receiving widespread newspaper and magazine coverage. Her previous titles have sold over a million copies worldwide, and include *Titania's Crystal Ball*, *Aroma Magic*, and *Hocus Pocus*. Her first novel is due to be published in summer 2007.

Acknowledgements

Many thanks to you, Nick, for the clear and brilliant vision; you knew what you wanted and, like a true and inspired **1**, kept mulling it over until a way was found. This is your baby. Also big thanks to Tessa, master number **22**, for your commitment to this magnum opùs beyond call: only you and I know, Tessa, how much time and soul has gone into all of these words. To Ian, for keeping us piping along with a true **4**'s sanguine approach to such a long body of work, and to Elaine and Malcolm for the look – **6**s, naturally! For my daughter Samantha, thanks for some of your ideas which found expression in the second-to-last section: I love the latte in Soho while signing the author. Let's see! To Georgia, for work in the field on number **5**, my thanks. To all of you, my appreciation, and I wish you all LUCKY NUMBERS!

EDDISON•SADD EDITIONS

Editorial Director **Ian Jackson**
Managing Editor **Tessa Monina**
Proofreader **Nikky Twyman**
Art Director **Elaine Partington**
Mac Designer **Malcolm Smythe**
Production **Sarah Rooney**